Lives of great men all remind us, we can make our lives sublime, and departing, leave behind us, footprints on the sands of time.
— Henry Wadsworth Longfellow

America's
LITERARY LEGENDS

Michael Thomas Barry

The Lives & Burial Places
of 50 Great Writers

4880 Lower Valley Road • Atglen, PA 19310

Dedication

This book is lovingly dedicated to my beautiful wife, Christyn.

Designed by Danielle D. Farmer
Type set in ITC Caslon 224 Std/Carol/P22 Cezanne Regular

ISBN: 978-0-7643-4702-3
Printed in China

Schiffer Books are available at special discounts for bulk purchases for sales promotions or premiums. Special editions, including personalized covers, corporate imprints, and excerpts can be created in large quantities for special needs. For more information contact the publisher:

Published by Schiffer Publishing, Ltd.
4880 Lower Valley Road
Atglen, PA 19310
Phone: (610) 593-1777; Fax: (610) 593-2002
E-mail: Info@schifferbooks.com

For the largest selection of fine reference books on this and related subjects, please visit our website at **www.schifferbooks.com**.

We are always looking for people to write books on new and related subjects. If you have an idea for a book, please contact us at proposals@schifferbooks.com.

This book may be purchased from the publisher.
Please try your bookstore first.
You may write for a free catalog.

Literary Legends of the British Isles: The Lives & Burial Places of 50 Great Writers | ISBN 978-0-7643-4438-1

Contents

Introduction 4

Part One:
THE CELEBRATED AUTHORS OF AMERICAN LITERATURE FROM COLONIAL TIMES THROUGH THE 19TH CENTURY

Washington Irving	10
James Fenimore Cooper	12
Ralph Waldo Emerson	15
Nathaniel Hawthorne	18
Henry Wadsworth Longfellow	22
Edgar Allan Poe	25
Oliver Wendell Holmes Sr.	29
Harriet Beecher Stowe	32
Henry David Thoreau	35
Herman Melville	38
Walt Whitman	41
Emily Dickinson	44
Louisa May Alcott	47
Mark Twain	49
Henry James	52
Stephen Crane	54

Part Two:
THE CELEBRATED AUTHORS OF AMERICAN LITERATURE IN THE 20TH CENTURY

L. Frank Baum	62
O. Henry	64
Edith Wharton	66
Theodore Dreiser	68
Willa Cather	71
Gertrude Stein	73
Robert Frost	76
Zane Grey	79
Edgar Rice Burroughs	82
Jack London	84
Carl Sandburg	87
Sinclair Lewis	89
Eugene O'Neill	91
Pearl S. Buck	93
E.E. Cummings	95
F. Scott Fitzgerald	97
William Faulkner	101

Thornton Wilder	104
Ernest Hemingway	106
E.B. White	112
Margaret Mitchell	114
John Steinbeck	116
Theodor Geisel "Dr. Seuss"	119
Robert Penn Warren	121
Tennessee Williams	123
Arthur Miller	126
J.D. Salinger	128
Ray Bradbury	131
Kurt Vonnegut	133
Jack Kerouac	135
Truman Capote	138
Flannery O'Connor	140
Sylvia Plath	142
John Updike	145

Conclusion 147

Bibliography 147

Index 153

How is greatness defined? *Merriam-Webster* defines "greatness" as remarkable in magnitude, degree, or effectiveness, and chief or preeminent over others. Greatness is an idea that centers on a condition of supremacy that often affects a person, object, or place. It is further defined to refer to individuals who own an unusual skill or talent that is better than all others. The perception of being great at something also carries the inference that the particular person or thing, when compared to others of a similar kind, skill, or talent, has an obvious advantage.

Given this definition of greatness, what is great literature? Is it something that has meaning and invokes thought? Is it defined by being likable, or achieving the author's goal? Is it marked by the span of time and influence that the story has, or is it a broad equation encompassing any or all—perhaps even none—of those characteristics? In this day and age where writing and book publication is prolific, effort alone cannot make a work great. The number of copies sold does not necessarily equate to a work being great or classic (although this used to be a good indicator). In the end, defining great literature is quite personal; it's like what makes art wonderful to one and horrid to another. To quote Irish author Margaret Wolfe Hungerford, "Beauty is in the eye of the beholder." In its simplest form, greatness, and in particular, great literature, can only be defined by its impact on others.

American literature spans nearly 300 years and in its broad sense has a little something for everyone: categories ranging from the romantic to the satirical, styles from the novel to the play, and authors ranging from illiterate storytellers to Nobel Prize winners. The lives of the people who wrote these iconic novels, poems, and plays are just as varied. The fifty writers included in this book most certainly penned some of the finest literature of all time and had an enormous impact on the world. One must first explore the historical context in which these authors wrote and the lives they lived, in order to better understand how and why they were able to write such enduring literary classics.

American literature is unrivaled both in its impact and in the fame of its authors. Trying to list everyone would be a tedious and almost impossible task. The intention of this book is to chronicle the lives and burial places of those commonly recognized to be the fifty most significant writers in American literary history. The sheer volume of great writers has led to some drastic cuts, and if your favorite has not been included, please accept my sincere apology. The life stories discussed within this volume are presented in chronological order and divided into two parts: nineteenth century and twentieth century. It is intended to be a companion piece to my previous book *Literary Legends of the British Isles: The Lives & Burial Places of 50 Great Writers*, which serves as an introductory study of the great writers of English literature.

Assembled within the following pages are an assortment of concise biographies—some splendid, a few pitiful, but all striking in their variety and improbable fates. Although there were many accomplished and noteworthy writers during the Colonial and post-Revolutionary War period, Washington Irving was chosen to begin this book because he is considered by most scholars to be the first author to support himself financially through his published works. As we examine the lives and works of these great men and women, it must be noted that ambition, great imagination, and the rejection of literary conventions made their lives and works groundbreaking. It is hoped that this collection of brief biographies will serve to promote further study into the lives and works of these legendary writers of American literature.

Part One

The Celebrated Authors of American Literature

From Colonial Times through the 19th Century

In tracing the development of American literature, we accept a common heritage with Chaucer, Milton, and Shakespeare of Great Britain, but this tradition does not imply finality, and our end is not to be found in the writings of the mother country. We assert the autonomous and natural advancement of American literature. To uncover the genesis of American literature, one has to look no further than England's great writers. It was they who passed the torch of prose and poetic light to Irving, Poe, Hawthorne, and Hemingway. When we turn over the pages of history and pause to reflect upon the landing of Captain John Smith on the southern shores of Virginia, this early period of American literature consisted of simple pamphlets. These works largely celebrated the positive benefits of the colonies to European readers. John Smith was the earliest source of such pamphlets and is considered by many to be the first American author. His works included: *A True Relation* (1608) and the *Generall Historie of Virginia, New England,* and the *Summer Isles (1624).*

When we follow the Puritans as they crossed the Atlantic and set foot upon the barren, desolate shores of Massachusetts in 1620, we know that this determined action was no fanatical whim, but was born of the spirit and courage of the times. From these two migrations sprang our heritage, and to follow the growth of American literature is to follow the North and South in the development of each in almost separate lines for nearly three centuries. To account for the marked difference is not to attribute it to its environment, as many have done, but to lineage. Virginia was not established, as some argue, by useless, worn-out aristocrats, or Massachusetts by religious fanatics. The descendants of Washington, Jefferson, Madison, Patrick Henry, and Henry Clay could not have been completely useless, and neither could ancestors of Irving, Emerson, and Hawthorne have all been narrow-minded extremists.

They arrived here frustrated with the church, the government, and all the institutions of the mother country. They sought to create for themselves a new church and government, but also came with loyalty to their former homeland. They planned to continue the traditions of their former institutions, public, political, and spiritual. The dissenters settled in the north and the loyalists settled in the south, and the influence of these two regions are evidenced in their distinct dialect and writing styles. The early writing of this period was not unique and can scarcely be called American. Even if it were so counted, it could not be called literature, for everyday chronicles help to make history, but not literature. These early settlers were too busy providing for everyday necessities of their new existence to find time for widespread reading or writing.

The significance of any country's literature is most often determined by its value, and not by its quantity. The Puritan lifestyle of the north was by nature optimistic and idealistic, and it was accepted that it should develop a great tradition of thinkers and writers. The southerner was viewed as a man of action and deeds, who was instrumental in the development of the statesman and orator, and was the colonizer of America. Each was as essential to building this nation as the other, and while it is commonly accepted that the North was a more fertile environment for the development of the majority of early authors, let it not be done to the denigration of the South, which also has contributed to the evolution of American literature.

Almost all literature derives from modest beginnings: diaries, journals, letters, sermons, travel logs, etc. During America's Colonial Period, these types of personal literature occupied a key position in the literary scene and mainly served religious purposes. In form, they were predominantly the imitations of earlier established English custom. Some important American writers of this period include the following:

. . . .

ANNE DUDLEY BRADSTREET (1612-1672) was one of the earliest noteworthy American poets. Her writings remained unrivaled by any other American woman writer until the emergence of Emily Dickinson in the 19th century. Bradstreet's *The Tenth Muse Lately Sprung Up in America* (1650) was the first published book of poetry written by an American colonist. She died on September 16, 1672, from tuberculosis. The exact location of her grave is unknown, but most historians agree that she is most likely buried at the Old North Burying Ground in North Andover, Massachusetts. A memorial cenotaph was placed there in 2000.

EDWARD TAYLOR (c. 1642-1729) wrote in the style of other metaphysical poets, such as John Donne and Samuel Johnson, whose works were often characterized by the creative use of exaggerated opinions about subjects, such as love or religion. Taylor's manuscripts were discovered in the 1930s. He died on June 29, 1729, in Westfield, Massachusetts, and his burial location is assumed to be at the Old Westfield Burying Ground in Westfield, Massachusetts.

[Left] Cotton Mather by Peter Pelham (circa 1700). Gravesite of Cotton Mather at Copps Hill Burying Ground, Boston, Massachusetts.

COTTON MATHER (1663-1728) was an influential New England minister whose pamphlets were filled with traditional references that attempted to reinvigorate the weakening Puritanical ideology of the period. His most well-known work was *Wonders of the Invisible World* (1693). Mather died on February 13, 1728, and was buried at Copps Hill Burying Ground in Boston, Massachusetts.

JOHN HECTOR ST. JOHN (1735-1813) was born in France and came to North America in 1755. His *Letters from an American Farmer* (1782) and *Journey into Northern Pennsylvania and the State of New York* (1801) served as one of the key contributors to the European understanding of American society during the late 18th and early 19th centuries. His essay "What is an American" became one of the most influential early reports on America. He died on November 12, 1813, in France. His burial location is unknown.

PHILLIS WHEATLEY (1754-1784) was the first significant African American poet. Born in Africa and sold into slavery, she was treated well by her masters and later gained her freedom. Her most significant work was *Poems on Various Subjects, Religious and Moral* (1773). She died on December 5, 1784, in Boston, Massachusetts, and was buried at Copps Hill Burying Ground.

Phillis Wheatley engraving by Scipio Moorhead (1773). *Courtesy of the Library of Congress, Prints & Photographs Division, LC-USZ62-12533.*

Portrait of Philip Freneau by Fredrick Halpin (1901) from *Philip Freneau, The Poet of the Revolution: A History of his Life and Times* by Mary S. Austin.

PHILIP FRENEAU (1752-1832) is commonly known as the "Poet of the American Revolution." His poetry blended neoclassicism and romanticism. His most famous poem, "The Rising Glory of America," was written in partnership with Hugh Henry Brackenridge. Freneau was also the founder of the *National Gazette*, a semi-weekly newspaper that became the voice of liberal democracy in American politics. He died on December 18, 1832, and was buried on a lot on Poet Road in Matawan, New Jersey. His grave inscription reads: "Heaven lifts its everlasting portal high and bids the pure in heart behold their god."

JONATHAN EDWARDS (1703-1758) is commonly recognized as America's most significant philosophical theologian and one of its earliest intellectuals. Edwards played a significant role in shaping the First Great Awakening and was the author of numerous books, including: *The Life of David Brainerd* (1749), which served to motivate thousands of missionaries throughout the 19th century. Edwards died on March 22, 1758, and was buried at the Princeton Cemetery in Princeton, New Jersey.

Theologian Jonathan Edwards engraving by R. Babson & J. Andrews (1855) in *The History of Connecticut, from the first settlement of the colony to the adoption of the present constitution* by G.H. Hollister (1855).

Benjamin Franklin's grave at Christ Church Burial Ground, Philadelphia, Pennsylvania.

[Left] Benjamin Franklin by Henry Bryan Hall (1879). *Courtesy of the Library of Congress, Prints & Photographs Division, LC-USZ62-90398.*

BENJAMIN FRANKLIN (1706-1790) was a printer, author, statesman, and inventor. He is considered by many scholars to be the father of the short story, with his "The Silence Dogood Papers." Franklin died on April 17, 1790, and was buried at the Christ Church Burial Ground in Philadelphia, Pennsylvania.

. . . .

As the American colonies moved closer to independence, the political writings of Samuel Adams, John Dickenson, Thomas Paine, and others took center stage. These writings would play an important role in influencing the political tone of the era. During the Revolution itself, poems and songs remained popular, and satirists, such as John Trumbull and Francis Hopkinson, wrote about the conflict. For some time after the American Revolution, our founding fathers and other intellectuals were too engaged in the details of nation-forming to devote attention to further developing any form of distinctly American literature. In the post-Revolutionary War period, American literature struggled to find a distinctive foothold in existing literary genres. European styles were often used and literary critics often viewed American authors as substandard. It was in the late 18th and early 19th centuries that America's first novels began to be published. *The Power of Sympathy* (1789) by William Hill Brown is generally considered to be the first American novel.

In the coming years, writers, such as Irving, Poe, Emerson, Thoreau, Hawthorne, Dickinson, Melville, and Whitman would emerge and would be instrumental in the development of modern *American* literature. Much like the colonial writers who had preceded them, the first writers in antebellum America largely followed British models. An early landmark in the history of American literature came in 1819, when Washington Irving published *The Sketch Book*, a collection of essays and stories that included "Rip Van Winkle" and "The Legend of Sleepy Hollow." A year later, fellow New Yorker James Fenimore Cooper published his first novel, *Precaution*. While the works of these two writers resembled the style of their English contemporaries in many ways, they also demonstrated two distinct differences. First, each writer, particularly Cooper in his *Leatherstocking Tales*, capitalized on uniquely American settings and themes. Second, both Irving and Cooper were more than inferior protégés; they were as talented as many of the British masters, and even earned the respect of European readers.

The next high point came in 1837 when Ralph Waldo Emerson delivered a lecture called "The American Scholar," which Oliver Wendell Holmes Sr. called America's "Intellectual Declaration of Independence." In the coming years, American writers produced numerous essays, nonfiction narratives, poems, short stories, and novels that helped form a distinctive American literature genre.

Much of early American literature still showed signs of British, or at least European, influence. Most conspicuously, Edgar Allan Poe wrote Gothic horror stories, many of which were set in European locales. Henry Wadsworth Longfellow often borrowed prose verse forms, and even subject matter, from his European counterparts, but his and Poe's writing was still clearly American in both form and content. In the areas of structure and method, Poe, along with Nathaniel Hawthorne and others, created a characteristically distinct American short story, and Walt Whitman developed a poetic form of free verse that was very different than European models. Both Hawthorne and Herman Melville wrote illustrative, even highly sophisticated, novels that differed from the works of their English contemporaries. In content, Emerson, Thoreau, Longfellow, Whitman, Cooper, Stowe, and Melville not only set works in American locales, but also relied upon unique American subjects and themes, including examination of democracy, individuality, slavery, Native Americans, and the frontier, while also lending their American perspectives to timeless subjects, such as nature, religion, and the search for truth in the universe.

In the years following the Civil War, American authors, unlike their antebellum predecessors, began to submerge themselves in the world around them. They traveled and came in close contact with real people, including some who were suffering the adverse effects of industrialization and urbanization.

Equally absorbed in the culture were writers whose works were published in magazines, such as *The Atlantic Monthly* and others. The experiences and perspectives of these writers helped shape the period's three major literary movements: realism, regionalism, and naturalism. Reacting against the pompous extravagance of literary romance, which told adventures of larger-than-life characters, realist writers, such as Mark Twain and Henry James, tried to depict life truthfully, rather than pretentiously. They depicted the dreams, desires, conflicts, and triumphs of their characters in a honest and humble fashion. The writers of regional fiction, called this "local color," strove for realism and often capitalized on the popularity of magazines, while other writers used details of landscape, dialect, and character to take readers to faraway American locations, such as the West, New Orleans, and the rural South. Finally, naturalism, which portrayed practical characters who struggled with societal issues, became popular in America due to journalistic efforts and the experiences of such writers as Jack London and Stephen Crane, who put their readers in touch with the struggles of everyday people from the lower-classes of society. This is the backdrop of the lives and works of some of the greatest writers of American literature during the 19th century.

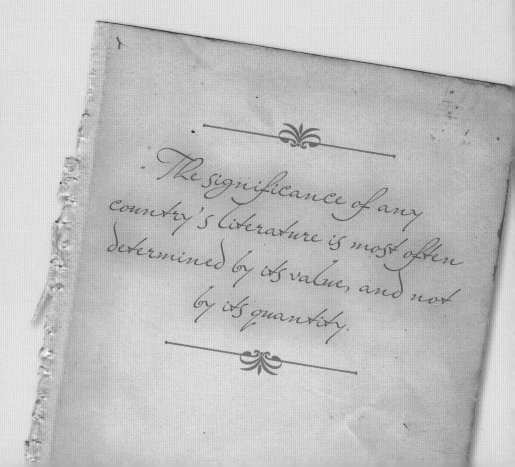

The significance of any country's literature is most often determined by its values, and not by its quantity.

Washington Irving
(1783–1859)

Washington Irving by Mathew Brady (1861). *Courtesy of the Library of Congress, Prints & Photographs Division, LC-USZ62-4238.*

NOVELIST, NON-FICTION WRITER & ESSAYIST

Born: New York City, New York

Died: Tarrytown, New York

Buried: Sleepy Hollow Cemetery, Tarrytown, New York

"Great minds have purposes; others have wishes."

WASHINGTON IRVING

Washington Irving is generally accepted to be the first "professional" writer in American literary history, and his clever use of the short story genre would help American literature gain respect within the international community. He would become America's first true literary celebrity and helped to establish a creative model that would be emulated by future generations of American short story writers. He was born on April 3, 1783, in New York City, the child of William Irving and Sarah Sanders. Named after President George Washington, Irving was an inquisitive and imaginative child, but found formal schooling quite boring. In early adulthood, he decided to go to work, rather than attend college. For relaxation and inspiration, he often traveled north to the Hudson River Valley. This region, located just north of New York City was known for its unique folklore and legends, and would later serve as a backdrop for many of his literary works.

In his late teens, Irving began writing letters to a variety of New York newspapers under an assortment of pseudonyms. In 1807, Irving, along with his brother, William, and personal friend, James Kirke Paulding, created the periodical, *Salmagundi*, in which they mocked New York's high society and politics. In 1809, Irving published his first book, *A History of New York, from the Beginning of the World to the End of the Dutch Dynasty*. The work was a humorously inaccurate account of New York's Dutch colonization. During this same period, Irving suffered personal tragedy when his fiancée, Matilda Hoffman, died unexpectedly. So affected by this tragic death, Irving would never marry. He later wrote about this lost love saying: "For years I could not talk on the subject of this hopeless regret; I could not even mention her name; but her image was continually before me, and I dreamt of her incessantly."

DID YOU KNOW?

Christmas and Santa Claus are relatively modern inventions in America. While one may think that Christmas has always been celebrated in this country and there has always been a Santa Claus, this is not so. Santa Claus, and the way we celebrate Christmas, was imported from British tradition by Washington Irving. His description of Santa, included in *History of New York* (1809), and his description of Christmas traditions in England in *The Sketchbook of Geoffrey Crayon*, have greatly influenced the way we observe the holiday. Before Irving's work came out, Christmas was not generally celebrated in the United States.

The Headless Horseman Pursuing Ichabod Crane (1858) by John Quidor. *Courtesy of the Smithsonian American Art Museum.*

Modern-day photograph of Washington Irving's home in Tarryton, New York.

Gravesite of Washington Irving at Sleepy Hollow Cemetery in Tarrytown, New York.

Following this tragedy, finding himself depressed and uninspired, Irving began to struggle in his literary career. In desperate need of a steady income, he found employment in his family's import-export business. By 1819, the company was closed and, as he found himself without any real means of financial support, Irving again turned to writing. He began compiling his thoughts and impressions into what would later become *The Sketch Book of Geoffrey Crayon*. This work was serially published between 1819-1820 and contained material that appealed to a wide range of readers. It included essays, travel pieces, and short stories, with the most famous stories being "Rip Van Winkle," "The Legend of Sleepy Hollow," and "The Spectre Bridegroom." The work was a financial and critical success in both the United States and Europe. Because of the financial success of *The Sketch Book*, Irving became the first American writer to support himself solely through his writing. He also became America's first international literary superstar.

In the decade following the release of *The Sketch Book*, Irving moved to Europe and continued to write and publish works, such as *Bracebridge Hall* or the *Humorists: A Medley* (1822). He then turned his attention from fiction writing to non-fiction. He traveled to Spain, where he lived for several years and wrote *The Life and Voyages of Christopher Columbus* (1828) and *The Chronicles of the Conquest of Granada* (1829). In 1830, he returned to the United States and began a tour of the West, but only ventured as far as Oklahoma. Irving chronicled this journey in a series of books that included *A Tour on the Prairies* (1835). He then bought some property near Tarrytown, New York, on the Hudson River, and built a home he called "Sunnyside."

During the last decade of his life, Irving continued to write, primarily publishing biographies of famous people. He wrote an extensive, five-volume biography of George Washington, which he worked on persistently, despite severe health issues, from the early 1850s until a few months before his death. On the evening of November 28, 1859, less than a year after finishing the final volume of this biography, Irving died from a heart attack at his home. Legend states that his last words were: "Well, I must arrange my pillows for another night. When will this end?" He was buried at Sleepy Hollow Cemetery and his final resting place was immortalized by Henry Wadsworth Longfellow in his poem, "In the Churchyard at Tarrytown" (1876). The poem concludes:

How sweet a life was his; how sweet a death!
Living, to wing with mirth the weary hours, or
with romantic tales the heart to cheer; Dying,
to leave a memory like the breath of summers
full of sunshine and of showers, a grief and
gladness in the atmosphere.

James Fenimore Cooper
(1789-1851)

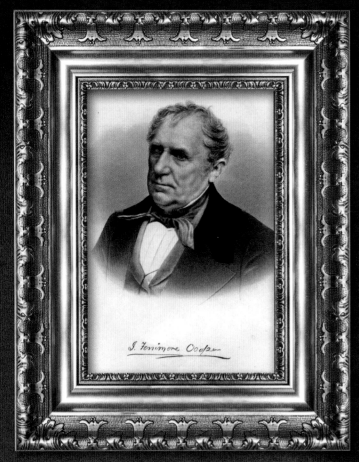

Engraving of James Fenimore Cooper (circa 1850) from a photograph by Matthew Brady.

NOVELIST

Born: Burlington, New Jersey

Died: Cooperstown, New York

Buried: Christ Episcopal Churchyard

Cooperstown, New York

"All greatness of character is dependent on individuality. The man who has no other existence than that which he partakes in common with all around him, will never have any other than an existence of mediocrity."

JAMES FENIMORE COOPER

James Fenimore Cooper is best remembered as a novelist whose romantic writings about Native Americans and the early frontier were instrumental in the development of American literature as a legitimate genre. He was born on September 15, 1789 in Burlington, New Jersey, the child of William Cooper and Elizabeth Fenimore. When James was an infant, his family moved to Cooperstown, New York, and his early childhood experiences in this tiny frontier town would provide him with a good foundation for his future literary endeavors.

Stereographic view of Otsego Hall by Washington G. Smith, circa 1865-1880.

In 1803, Cooper began attending Yale College in New Haven, Connecticut, but was expelled two years later for involvement in a practical joke that went astray. After leaving college, Cooper found employment as a sailor on a merchant ship. He traveled to many exotic locations, and his lifelong love for the sea would be a subject of many of his future literary works. He joined the United States Navy as midshipman in 1809, but after only a few months of duty, had to resign following the untimely death of his father. Returning home, Cooper tried his hand at farming and began to consider a career in writing. On January 1, 1811, he married Susan Augusta De Lancey. They would have seven children together and one daughter, Susan Fenimore Cooper, would also become a writer. She helped edit many of her father's literary works.

Cooper began to write after moving to Scarsdale, New York, in the early 1820s. He published his first novel, *Precaution*, in 1820, which was panned by critics and sold poorly. Legend states that Cooper wrote this book after being challenged by his wife. His biographer Warren Walker wrote: "In the customary practice of the day he was reading aloud to his wife one evening from a current English novel, but found the story dull. Throwing it aside, he declared, 'I could write a better book than that myself.' And Susan's challenge to make good his boast resulted in his writing *Precaution*."

His next work, *The Spy: A Tale of Neutral Ground* (1821), was a critical and financial hit and, because of this success, Cooper was determined to pursue a full-time career as a writer and moved to New York City. There he quickly became a prominent member of the city's social elite and went on to write *The Pioneers* (1823), which would eventually become one of a series

of five novels collectively entitled *The Leatherstocking Tales*. This collection of books became the first financially successful American novel series.

At the apex of his literary fame, Cooper traveled to Europe on what would be a seven-year adventure. During this period, he wrote numerous books, including: *The Prairie and Notions of the Americans*, and three historical novels that resembled the writing of Sir Walter Scott. Cooper returned to the United States in 1833, and soon became disillusioned with America's narrow-mindedness and customs. He then began to write the controversial *A Letter to his Countrymen* (1834). After the book's release in 1834, Copper became embroiled in numerous disputes in which he was labeled by several newspapers as being a false aristocrat who had become disillusioned with American ideals through European influences. Cooper responded to these accusations by filing lawsuits, which were successful in setting legal precedents against what personal information the press could release.

"Bear Hug," from an 1896 edition of *The Last of the Mohicans* illustrated by F.T. Merrill.

In the last decade of his life, Cooper wrote numerous novels and assorted non-fiction works, such as: *The American Democrat* (1838), *The Last of the Mohicans* (1826), *The History of the Navy of the United States of America* (1839), *The Pathfinder* (1840), *The Deerslayer* (1841), and *The Distinguished American Naval Officers* (1846). He died on September 14, 1851, at his home in Cooperstown, New York, from edema (which is an abnormal accumulation of fluid beneath the skin). Cooper was buried within the family plot at the Christ Episcopal Churchyard Cemetery in Cooperstown. His wife, Susan, survived him by only a few months and was laid to rest beside him.

In the decade prior to his death, Cooper was more respected in Europe than in America and had a great influence on writers Honore de Balzac, Leo Tolstoy, and many others. Cooper's writing has often been criticized as being overly romantic and too educational, but his contributions to early American fiction are undeniable. Many people would be surprised to learn how Cooper's innovative writing style and ideas have helped shape the writing of so many authors.

1– Gravesite of James Fenimore Cooper and his wife at Christ Episcopal Churchyard, Cooperstown, New York.

2– Close-up of James Fenimore Cooper's grave marker.

3– Statue of James Fenimore Cooper at Cooperstown, New York.

> "*If well-used books are among the best of all things, abused are among the worst.*"

RALPH WALDO EMERSON

Ralph Waldo Emerson, circa 1884. *Courtesy of the Library of Congress, Prints & Photographs Division, LC-USZ62-116399.*

RALPH WALDO EMERSON
(1803-1882)

Ralph Waldo Emerson was a staunch defender of individuality and was a founding member of the Transcendentalist movement of the mid-19th century. Emerson used the written word and public lectures to spread his opinions. He wrote on many subjects, and often advocated for individuality and liberty. He was born on May 25, 1803, in Boston, Massachusetts, to Unitarian minister William Emerson and his wife, Ruth Haskins. He was raised in a strict, but loving, household. His father died in 1811, and this would be only the first of many tragic deaths of relatives and friends. Following his father's death, Ralph became closer to his mother, siblings, and other relatives, all of whom would have a constructive influence on his intellectual development. As a child, Emerson began to write down his thoughts and observations in journals. These early writings would later serve as the foundation for many of his most famous essays. While his later writings were often criticized as being too theoretical, he was almost universally praised for his eloquent speaking ability.

In 1817, at the age of fourteen, Emerson began attending Harvard College's School of Divinity. He graduated in 1821, and wrote his first essay, "Thoughts on the Religion of the Middle Ages," which was published in *The Christian Disciple* in 1822. Six years later, he accepted a position as pastor of Boston's Second Church, but left the position in 1832 because of personal conflicts with religious doctrine and practices. During this same period, Emerson met his first wife, Ellen Louisa Tucker, and they were married on September 30, 1829. At this time, she was already beginning to show early symptoms of tuberculosis, and she died on February 8, 1831. After her death, Emerson fell into a deep depression and was overcome by a wave of religious questioning and doubt. He visited her grave at the Roxbury Burying Ground in Boston on a daily basis. In 1878, Ellen's remains were re-interred at Mt. Auburn Cemetery in Cambridge, Massachusetts, with that of her family.

In the years following his wife's death, Emerson began to travel and visited many different locations throughout Europe. On these travels, he met numerous writers and intellectuals, including Thomas Carlyle, Samuel Taylor Coleridge, and William Wordsworth. Carlyle, in particular, would have a unique influence on Emerson, and they

POET, ESSAYIST & LECTURER

Born: Boston, Massachusetts

Died: Concord, Massachusetts

Buried: Sleepy Hollow Cemetery

Concord, Massachusetts

The Old Manse, the ancestral home of the Emerson family in Concord, Massachusetts. In November 1834, Ralph Waldo Emerson moved here to live with his aging step-grandfather Ezra Ripley. While there, he wrote the first draft of "Nature," a foundational work of the Transcendentalist movement.

DID YOU KNOW?

Emerson's emphasis on transcendence sometimes came at the cost of reality. When Emerson visited the dying Nathaniel Hawthorne and found him too frail to pull on his own boots, he lectured him about inner strength instead of just helping his sick friend put his shoes on.

would remain close friends and confidants until Carlyle's death in 1881. Emerson returned to the United States in the fall of 1833, and first settled in Newton, Massachusetts, later moving to Concord, Massachusetts, to live with his step-grandfather Dr. Ezra Ripley at "The Old Manse."

At this point, Emerson began to follow the teachings of Josiah Holbrook, the founder of the American Lyceum Movement. Holbrook was a passionate advocate for the improvement of conversation, providing good education for children, and the support of public libraries. His organization would host educational lectures throughout New England and proved to be very popular. On November 5, 1833, Emerson made the first of what would eventually become over 1,500 lectures. In this address, he discussed ideas and beliefs that would later become his first essay, "Nature" (1836).

In March 1834, Emerson met Lydia Jackson of Plymouth, Massachusetts. They married on September 14, 1835, and had four children, settling in Concord, Massachusetts, where they would live for the remainder of their lives. At his home in Concord, Emerson would often entertain fellow Transcendentalists, such as Henry David Thoreau, Nathaniel Hawthorne, Bronson Alcott, and Alcott's daughter, Louisa May Alcott. Thoreau would build his Walden Pond cabin on property that was owned by Emerson.

On July 15, 1838, at Harvard College, Emerson delivered what many considered to be his most contentious speech. In his "Divinity School Address," Emerson discussed what he labeled the failures of historical Christianity. He spoke on the differences between radical Transcendentalist thought and conventional Unitarian theology, and argued that truthful observation was a better guide to morality than religious principle. He also discounted the necessity of belief in the historical miracles of Jesus and questioned the philosophical legitimacy of such church tenets as Holy Communion. Emerson believed that this ritual, among others, was inconsistent with the original teachings of Jesus. He was shocked at the extent of negative criticism that followed this address. The Unitarian establishment of New England and scholars of the Harvard Divinity School rejected his ideas completely.

The Transcendentalist movement of which Emerson would become a leading advocate had begun as a protest of the broad state of cultural and intellectual decline in the United States. Chief among the core beliefs of the Transcendentalists was the thought that goodness was an inherent trait in all humanity, but that society and all of its manmade institutions, such as organized religion and political parties, would ultimately distort the natural integrity of the individual. In 1840, Emerson, along with Margaret Fuller, began to publish the Transcendentalist publication *The Dial*. This periodical would serve as the official publication of the movement for the next four years.

Many of Emerson's early essays would be published within the pages of *The Dial*, including compilations, such as *First Series* (1841). This collection of essays would include some of his most iconic writings, such as "Self-Reliance, Love, Friendship, and Prudence." Over the next thirty years, he would publish numerous writings collections: Essays: *Second Series* (1844), *Poems* (1847), *Miscellanies: Embracing Nature, Addresses, and Lectures* (1849), *Representative Men* (1850), *The Conduct of Life* (1860), *May-Day and Other Pieces* (1867), and *Society and Solitude* (1870).

By the late 1860s, Emerson began to develop health issues, including memory loss, which greatly affected his literary output and ability to give lectures. On July 24, 1872, tragedy struck when his Concord home was destroyed by a fire. The physical and psychological effects of this disaster effectively ended Emerson's lecturing career. In late 1874, Emerson published an anthology of poetry called *Parnassus*, which included poems by Henry David Thoreau and others. By 1879, his health issues had become so pronounced that all future public appearances were canceled. On April 27, 1882, Emerson died from pneumonia at his home in Concord and was buried at Sleepy Hollow Cemetery. He was placed in his coffin wearing a white robe given by American sculptor Daniel Chester French. Lydia Emerson survived her husband by ten years, and both now rest beside one another on Author's Ridge, not far from friends and fellow writers, such as Nathaniel Hawthorne, Louisa May Alcott, and Henry David Thoreau.

1– Home of Ralph Waldo Emerson in Concord, Massachusetts, from 1835 until his death in 1882. Today, the home is still owned by the Emerson family. It is run as a private museum and is a registered historic landmark.

2– Gravesite of Ralph Waldo Emerson on Author's Ridge at Sleepy Hollow Cemetery, Concord, Massachusetts. His final resting place is marked by a large boulder, which is flanked on the left by his wife's grave and to the right by his daughter, Ellen's.

Nathaniel Hawthorne
(1804-1864)

Nathaniel Hawthorne, photograph by Matthew Brady, circa 1860-1864.
Courtesy of the Library of Congress, Prints & Photographs Division, LC-DIG-CWPBH-03440.

NOVELIST & SHORT STORY WRITER

Born: Salem, Massachusetts

Died: Plymouth, New Hampshire

Buried: Sleepy Hollow Cemetery

Concord, Massachusetts

"Words – so innocent and powerless as they are, as standing in a dictionary, how potent for good and evil they become in the hands of one who knows how to combine them."

NATHANIEL HAWTHORNE

Nathaniel Hawthorne was one of the most popular and innovative writers of his era. His works were often mysterious and disturbing. He often explored the ideas of individual responsibility, the importance of creative expression, and man's relationship to the natural world. Nathaniel Hathorne Jr. (he would later add the "w" to the family name) was born on July 4, 1804, in Salem, Massachusetts, the son of Nathaniel Hathorne and Elizabeth Clarke Manning. His ancestors included many prominent New England Puritans who had been involved in religious persecution. One of his relatives, John Hathorne, was one of the three judges who presided over the infamous Salem Witch Trials of the late seventeenth century. Shortly after graduating from college, Nathaniel, in an effort to distance himself from his infamous ancestor, changed the spelling of his surname to Hawthorne.

Nathaniel Hawthorne's birthplace in Salem, Massachusetts.

Nathaniel's father was a sea captain and, in 1808, died from yellow fever in Suriname, leaving his wife and three children destitute and dependent on relatives for support. For the next ten years, Nathaniel, his mother, and two sisters lived with relatives in Salem. During this time, young Nathaniel sustained a leg injury and was bedridden for almost a year, though physicians could not find any physical ailment. With the financial backing of a wealthy relative, Hawthorne was able to attend Bowdoin College (1821-1825), where he excelled at English composition. Fellow classmates included Henry Wadsworth Longfellow and future U.S. President Franklin Pierce.

After graduating in 1825, Hawthorne returned home to live with his mother in Salem. He would often reflect on these twelve years (1825-1837) as a time of dreamlike isolation and solitude. It was during this period that Hawthorne began to write. Recent biographers have shown that this period was less lonely than he remembered it to be, and, in truth, Hawthorne was quite social.

Most of Hawthorne's early works were published anonymously in magazines. He was encouraged to collect these previously anonymous stories by a friend, who offered to finance the cost of publication. When the works became popular, a review in the *Boston Post* revealed Hawthorne was the author.

The title of his *Twice-Told Tales* was based on a line from William Shakespeare's *The Life and Death of King John*. The book was published by the American Stationers' Company on March 6, 1837. After this book's publication, Hawthorne asked a friend to check with the local bookstore to see how it was selling. After noting that the initial expenses for publishing had not yet been met, Hawthorne complained: "Surely the book was puffed enough to meet with sale. What the devil's the matter?"

By June, only 700 copies had been sold, but sales were soon halted completely when the publisher went out of business. Hawthorne was struggling financially and it was suggested that he buy back unsold copies of *Twice-Told Tales* so that they could be reissued through a different publisher. By 1844, there were 600 unsold copies of the book and Hawthorne lamented, "I wish Heaven would make me rich enough to buy the copies for the purpose of burning them."

After the success of *The Scarlet Letter* in 1850, *Twice-Told Tales* was reissued with the help of publisher James Thomas Fields. In a new preface, Hawthorne wrote that the stories "may be understood and felt by anybody, who will give himself the trouble to read it, and will take up the book in a proper mood."

Following the republication of *Twice-Told Tales*, Hawthorne wrote *Grandfather's Chair* (1841), *Mosses from an Old Manse* (1846), and *The Snow-Image* (1851). Ultimately, his short stories came into critical favor, and the best of them have become American classics. By his own account, it was Hawthorne's love of his Salem neighbor, Sophia Peabody, who brought him from his "haunted chamber" out into the world. His books were far from profitable, so, in 1838, he went to work in the Boston Custom House and spent part of 1841 at the Transcendentalist Utopian community at Brook Farm. He left later that year, as he realized he did not agree with the community's ideals, though his Brook Farm adventure would prove an inspiration for his later novel, *The Blithedale Romance* (1852).

Sophia Peabody Hawthorne (1808-1871) from an engraving by S.A. Schoff in *Nathaniel Hawthorne and His Wife: A Biography* by Julian Hawthorne (1884).

On July 9, 1842, Hawthorne married Sophia Peabody in Boston. Like Hawthorne, Sophia was an introvert and a recluse. Throughout her early life, she suffered severe health issues that included frequent migraines for which she attempted to alleviate with experimental medical treatments. Hawthorne was first introduced to his future wife through her sister, Elizabeth. When Nathaniel first came to visit the Peabody home, Sophia was urged to come downstairs to meet him, but she refused stating, "If he has come once, he will come again." Sophia had originally objected to marriage, partly because of her health, but she and Nathaniel were secretly engaged on New Year's Day 1839.

At the time of their wedding, both Hawthorne and Peabody were considered relatively old for marriage (she was 32 and he was 38), but their union proved to very happy. Soon after the wedding, the Hawthornes moved to Concord, Massachusetts. Of his wife, whom he referred to as his "dove," Hawthorne wrote that she "is, in the strictest sense, my sole companion; and I need no other, there is no vacancy in my mind, any more than in my heart...Thank God that I suffice for her boundless heart!" Together they would have three children.

In Concord, Hawthorne was the neighbor of Ralph Waldo Emerson, who invited him into his social circle, which included Henry David Thoreau, poet Ellery Channing, and others. At the Old Manse, Hawthorne wrote most of the short stories for *Mosses from an Old Manse* (1852). In 1846, he was appointed to the position of surveyor in the Salem Custom House and had great difficulty writing. He confided to Henry Wadsworth Longfellow: "I am trying to resume my pen... Whenever I sit alone, or walk alone, I find myself dreaming about stories, as of old; but these forenoons in the Custom House undo all that the afternoons and evenings have done. I should be happier if I could write." Like most other political appointments, this position was vulnerable to political whims of those in power. A Democrat, Hawthorne lost this job due to the change of administration in Washington after the presidential election of 1848. His dismissal, however, turned out to be a blessing, since it gave him time to write his greatest novel, *The Scarlet Letter* (1850).

The novel, set in 17th century Boston, tells the story of Hester Prynne, who conceives a daughter through an affair and struggles to create a new life of atonement in a hostile and unforgiving puritanical environment. The book's immediate and lasting success has been credited to its use of spiritual and moral issues, which were addressed from a uniquely American standpoint. In 1850, the subject of adultery was considered taboo, but because Hawthorne had the support of the New England literary establishment, it passed easily into the realm of appropriate reading.

Hester Prynne & Pearl before the stocks, an engraved illustration from the 1878 edition of Hawthorne's *The Scarlet Letter*.

House of the Seven Gables in Salem, Massachusetts. This home was the inspiration behind Hawthorne's novel, *The House of the Seven Gables*.

The period from 1850 to 1853 was Hawthorne's most productive as an author, as he wrote *The House of the Seven Gables* (1851), *The Blithedale Romance* (1852), *A Wonder Book* (1852), and *Tanglewood Tales* (1853). Hawthorne and his family moved to a small farmhouse near Lenox, Massachusetts, at the end of March 1850. There he formed a meaningful friendship with fellow novelist Herman Melville.

That same year, Hawthorne wrote the biography of his college friend Franklin Pierce, entitled *The Life of Franklin Pierce*. The biography depicted Pierce as a man of peaceful pursuits, with few or no personal flaws. He intentionally left out Pierce's drinking habits, despite rumors of his alcoholism, and emphasized Pierce's belief that slavery could not "be remedied by human contrivances" but would, over time, "vanish like a dream."

When Pierce was elected President, Hawthorne was rewarded for his loyalty with an appointment as United States consul in Liverpool, which was considered to be one of the

Nathaniel Hawthorne's home, "Wayside" in Concord, Massachusetts. The home was the home of three authors: Hawthorne, Louisa May Alcott, and Margaret Sidney.

Gravesite of Nathaniel Hawthorne at Sleepy Hollow Cemetery in Concord, Massachusetts.

most lucrative Foreign Service positions. In 1857, his appointment ended at the close of the Pierce administration, and the Hawthorne family toured France and Italy. They returned to the United States in 1860 and took up residence in their first permanent home, The Wayside, in Concord, Massachusetts. That same year, Hawthorne finished his last and longest complete novel, *The Marble Faun* (1860).

As Hawthorne began to age, his health began to steadily decline. He refused to submit to any thorough medical examination, thus the details of his ailments have remained a mystery. In May of 1864, Hawthorne, who was suffering from numerous maladies, insisted on taking a recuperative trip to New Hampshire with his friend, former President Franklin Pierce.

Hawthorne died in his sleep on May 19, 1864, while on a tour of the White Mountains in Plymouth, New Hampshire. He was buried at Sleepy Hollow Cemetery in Concord, Massachusetts, on what is now known as Author's Ridge. Pallbearers at his funeral included Henry Wadsworth Longfellow, Ralph Waldo Emerson, Oliver Wendell Holmes, James Thomas Fields, Edwin Percy Whipple, and Bronson Alcott. Emerson later wrote of the funeral: "I thought there was a tragic element in the event, that might be more fully rendered, in the painful solitude of the man, which, I suppose, could no longer be endured, and he died of it."

After her husband's death, Sophia moved to England with their three children. On February 26, 1871, she became ill and died from typhoid fever. Sophia Hawthorne was buried at Kensal Green Cemetery in London. Their daughter, Una, died in September 1877 and was buried alongside her mother. One hundred years later, their gravesites were in need of costly repair, and it was suggested that their remains be moved to the Hawthorne family plot in Concord, Massachusetts. In June 2006, Sophia and Una Hawthorne were re-buried alongside Nathaniel at Sleepy Hollow Cemetery.

Henry Wadsworth Longfellow
(1807-1882)

Henry Wadsworth Longfellow on the Isle of Wight, England, in 1868 by Julia Margaret Cameron.

POET

Born: Portland, Maine

Died: Cambridge, Massachusetts

Buried: Auburn Cemetery, Cambridge, Massachusetts

"Lives of great men all remind us, we can make our lives sublime, and, departing, leave behind us, footprints on the sands of time."

HENRY WADSWORTH LONGFELLOW

Henry Wadsworth Longfellow was the most popular American poet of his day. He primarily wrote lyric poems, which were known for their musicality, but was criticized for imitating European styles and writing specifically for the masses. He was born on February 27, 1807, in Portland, Maine, the second child of Stephen Longfellow and Zilpah Wadsworth. After Henry's birth, the family moved to a house on Congress Street, now known as the Wadsworth Longfellow Home. From an early age, Henry knew he wanted to be a poet; he was a fast learner and loved to write. The *Portland Gazette* printed his first poem at the age of thirteen. Henry and his siblings often visited their grandparents' farm, and he reveled in the natural beauty of the nearby shores of Casco Bay. The bustling comings and goings of the port city fed his imagination.

Longfellow's birthplace, Portland, Maine (circa 1910-1920). *Courtesy of the Library of Congress, Prints & Photographs Division, LC-D4-72586.*

Birthplace of Henry Wadsworth Longfellow.

In 1822, Longfellow began attending Bowdoin College in Brunswick, Maine, and it was during this time that he befriended Nathaniel Hawthorne with whom he would remain lifelong friends. During these early years, Longfellow would write dozens of minor poems, many of which would be published in popular literary magazines. He graduated in 1825, and was offered a professorship of modern languages at Bowdoin, but the appointment was conditional upon him traveling to Europe to study French, Spanish, and Italian. During his three-year tour of Europe, Longfellow immersed himself in the literature of the continent and mastered half-a-dozen languages. He arrived back in the United States in August of 1829 and began his teaching assignment at Bowdoin. There he taught modern languages, including French and Italian, from 1829-1835. During his years teaching at the college, Longfellow translated numerous textbooks in French, Italian, and Spanish; his first published book was in 1833, a translation of the poetry of medieval Spanish poet Jorge Manrique. He also published a travel book, *Outre-Mer: A Pilgrimage Beyond the Sea* (1835).

Longfellow married longtime friend Mary Storer Potter on September 14, 1831, and the couple then moved to Brunswick, Maine. Two years later, he published several poems including "The Indian Summer" and "The Bald Eagle." In December 1834, he was offered a professorship at Harvard College with the provision that he spend another year abroad studying. On November 29, 1835, Mary suffered a miscarriage and died. Longfellow was distraught and wrote, "One thought occupies me night and day...she is dead, she is dead! All day I am weary and sad." Three years later, to honor his wife, he wrote the poem "Footsteps of Angels" (1838). Longfellow had Mary's body shipped to Boston, and buried at Mount Auburn Cemetery in Cambridge, Massachusetts. Arriving back in the United States in 1836, Longfellow began his assignment at Harvard teaching modern languages, a position he would hold for nearly twenty years.

Following a lengthy courtship, Longfellow married Francis Elizabeth "Fanny" Appleton on July 13, 1843, and, together, they would have six children. She was a talented artist, well-traveled, and well-read in many subjects. As a wedding gift, Fanny's father bought the couple "Craigie House" in Cambridge. During this period, Longfellow continued to write poetry and published such classics as *Voices of the Night: Ballads; and other Poems* (1839), *Hyperion, a Romance* (1839), *Ballads and Other Poems* (1841), and *Poems on Slavery* (1842). In 1854, he resigned from Harvard and devoted all his creative energies to writing. The following year, he penned one of his most famous works, *The Song of Hiawatha*, an epic poem based on Native American legends. This poem showed Longfellow at his very best, and other extraordinary works to follow included *The Courtship of Miles Standish and Other Poems* (1858) and a translation of *Dante's Divine Comedy* (1861).

Tragedy struck on July 9, 1861, when Fanny was severely injured after being burned. How the accident occurred is uncertain. Longfellow muffled the flames as best he could, but she was already severely burned. She died shortly after 10 o'clock the next morning. Longfellow's

Fanny Appleton Longfellow, with sons Charles and Ernest, circa 1849.

youngest daughter, Annie, claimed that the fire had started from a self-lighting match that had fallen on the floor and ignited Mrs. Longfellow's dress. Longfellow was unable to attend the funeral because of his own injuries and, for the remainder of his life, he was forced to grow a beard to hide them. Devastated by his wife's death, he never fully recovered from the tragedy and often resorted to drug use to deal with the mental and physical trauma of the incident. In 1879, eighteen years after the accident, Longfellow wrote *The Cross of Snow*, to commemorate his wife's death. In the coming years, he continued to write and published such works as *Tales of a Wayside Inn* (1863), *Household Poems* (1865), and *Flower-de-Luce* (1867). The same year that *The New England Tragedies* (1868) was published, he embarked on a final journey to Europe.

Longfellow continued to write poetry until the year of his death. His last works include *Three Books of Song* (1872), *Kéramos and Other Poems* (1878), and *In the Harbor* (1882). On Friday, March 24, 1882, Longfellow died surrounded by family at his home in Cambridge, Massachusetts. He had been suffering from peritonitis, an inflammation of the inner wall of the abdomen and was buried with both of his wives at Mount Auburn Cemetery in Cambridge. His last few years were spent translating the poetry of Michelangelo. Though Longfellow never considered it complete enough to be published during his lifetime, it was posthumously published in 1883. The following year, he became the first American author to be honored with a memorial within Poets' Corner at Westminster Abbey.

1- Longfellow House, Cambridge, Massachusetts.

2- Henry Wadsworth Longfellow's gravesite at Auburn Cemetery, Cambridge, Massachusetts.

"Words have no power to impress the mind without the exquisite horror of their reality."

EDGAR ALLAN POE

Edgar Allan Poe never achieved financial success during his lifetime, but has become one of American literature's most beloved authors. Poe is known for his innovative short stories of horror and mystery and is considered one of the pioneers of the American Romantic movement. He is also considered to be the creator of the detective novel and works, such as *The Raven* (1845) are considered classics of American literature. The details of Poe's life, much like his stories, have become somewhat of a mystery, with fact and fiction often being distorted since his death.

He was born on January 19, 1809, in Boston, Massachusetts, the son of David Poe and Elizabeth Arnold Hopkins. His father quickly deserted the family and his mother died from tuberculosis when Edgar was only two. Following his mother's death, Edgar was sent to live with John Allan in Richmond, Virginia. The Allans would serve as his foster family and gave him his middle name, but never officially adopted him. In 1815, the Allans traveled to England and Edgar was sent to school in Scotland. After one year, he rejoined the family in London. In 1820, the family moved back to Richmond, Virginia.

In 1826, Poe began attending the University of Virginia, but had to withdraw after a year. He amassed huge gambling debts and soon became estranged from his foster father. Poe would later claim that he had to leave school because Mr. Allan had not given him sufficient funds to register for classes and other expenses. In reality, Allan had sent his foster son enough money for school expenses, but Edgar had squandered it on gambling. Mr. Allan felt he had no choice but to cut Edgar off from further funding. With no other option, Poe was forced to leave college and return home, but quickly decided to travel to Boston.

Edgar Allan Poe. *Courtesy of the Library of Congress, Prints & Photographs Division, LC-USZ62-10610.*

POET, SHORT STORY WRITER, & NOVELIST

Born: Boston, Massachusetts

Died: Baltimore, Maryland

Buried: Old Westminster Burying Ground of Baltimore, Maryland

Edgar Allan Poe's birthplace marker in Boston, Massachusetts.

Edgar Allan Poe's birthplace in Boston, Massachusetts.

Unable to financially support himself, he enlisted in the army and, later that same year, published his first book of poetry, *Tamerlane and Other Poems* (1857). Poe disliked life in the army and after only two years, asked for an early discharge from his five-year obligation. However, his discharge was contingent upon a reconciliation with his foster father. Several months passed and Edgar's pleas to Mr. Allan went unanswered. Softened by Mrs. Allan's death on February 28, 1829, John Allan agreed to support his foster son's early discharge from the army conditional upon his acceptance of an appointment to the U.S. Military Academy at West Point. Edgar accepted this agreement and was discharged from the army in April 1829. Prior to leaving for West Point, Poe traveled to Baltimore to visit his aunt, Maria Clemm, and her young daughter, Virginia Eliza. During this period, Poe published a second book of poetry, *Al Aaraaf, Tamerlane and Minor Poems* (1829).

He arrived at West Point in July 1830 and soon began officers' training. Later that same year, John Allan married Louisa Patterson. Poe was opposed to the marriage and bitterly quarreled with his foster father. These arguments eventually led to Allan disowning his foster son. In an act of rebellion, Poe made the rash decision to leave West Point by being purposely kicked out of the academy. On February 8, 1831, he was tried and found guilty of gross neglect of duty and disobedience of orders and was dismissed from the academy. Soon after, he left for New York City and released a third volume of poems, which was financed with help from his fellow cadets at West Point.

After being dismissed from West Point, Poe returned to Baltimore to live with the Clemms. There he was reunited with his teenage cousin, Virginia, who became his literary muse, as well as a love interest. Poe and Virginia Clemm (who was only 13) were married on May 16, 1836. They moved to Richmond, where Poe was hired as a literary reviewer for *The Southern Literary Messenger* and quickly developed a reputation as a ruthless critic, writing brutally honest reviews of his colleagues. He also published some of his own works in the magazine, including two parts of his only novel, *The Narrative of Arthur Gordon Pym* (1838). Because of his combative personality and strained relationship with editors, along with bouts of alcoholism, Poe was forced to leave the magazine in 1837. He then found brief employment with two other periodicals, *Burton's Gentleman's Magazine* and *The Broadway Journal*. He published a collection of short stories, *Tales of the Grotesque and Arabesque* (1840) that included several of his most famous stories, such as "The Fall of the House of Usher" and "Ligeia." The book received mixed reviews and had limited financial success.

In 1841, Poe published what is considered by many to be the first detective story, "The Murders in the Rue Morgue." That same year, he submitted a short story entitled "The Gold-Bug" to a writing contest sponsored by the *Philadelphia Dollar Newspaper*. The story won the contest and was published in three installments beginning in June 1843. "The Gold-Bug" was an instant success and became one of Poe's most popular and widely read works during his lifetime.

Edgar Allan Poe lived in this house on 7th Avenue in Philadelphia, Pennsylvania from 1843-1844.

Poe spent the last few years of his life in this small cottage located at Kingsbridge Road and the Grand Concourse in The Bronx, New York. Virginia Poe died in the cottage's first floor bedroom on January 30, 1847.

In January 1842, Virginia Poe began to show early symptoms of tuberculosis. Because of his wife's prognosis, Poe became severely depressed and began to drink heavily. He returned to New York, where he worked briefly at the *Evening Mirror* before becoming editor of the *Broadway Journal*. On January 29, 1845, Poe published *The Raven* in the *Evening Mirror*. Its publication made Poe very popular in his lifetime, although it did not bring him much financial success. This poem is considered by many to be one of the greatest works of American literature and contains themes, such as death and loss, and it is celebrated for its musicality, stylized language, and paranormal tone. Poe claimed to have written the poem logically and methodically, intending to create a poem that would appeal to both critical and popular tastes. He claimed the poem was inspired, in part, by a talking raven in the novel *Barnaby Rudge* by Charles Dickens.

Following the folding of the *Broadway Journal* in 1846, Poe moved to The Bronx, New York, where Virginia Poe died on January 30, 1847, after suffering from tuberculosis for several years. Although overcome with grief, Poe continued to write, but the remaining years of his life were filled with poor health and financial hardships. His last days remain somewhat of a mystery. He left Richmond, Virginia, on September 27, 1849, for Philadelphia, but was found in Baltimore on the 3rd of October in great distress. He was taken to Washington College Hospital, where he died on October 7, 1849, never regaining full consciousness. He is reported to have repeatedly called out the name "Reynolds" on the night before his death, though it is unclear to whom he was referring. Some sources say Poe's final words were: "Lord help my poor soul." All medical records, including his death certificate, have been lost. Newspapers at the time reported Poe's death to be caused by congestion of the brain or cerebral inflammation, common euphemisms at the time for deaths from scandalous causes, such as alcoholism.

Poe was originally buried in an unmarked grave at the Old Westminster Burying Ground of Baltimore. On the day of his burial, an obituary appeared in the *New York Tribune*; it read in part: "Edgar Allan Poe is dead. He died in Baltimore the day before yesterday. This announcement will startle many, but few will be grieved by it." The anonymous writer of the obituary was later identified as Rufus Wilmot Griswold, a critic who harbored a long grudge against Poe. Ironically, Griswold would later become Poe's literary executor and continue to deliberately destroy his reputation. He would also write an article that was included in an 1850 volume of Poe's collected works. In this piece, Griswold depicted Poe as an immoral drunk and drug-induced madman. Many of these claims were either complete lies or distorted half-truths. Griswold's book was denounced by Poe's closest associates and friends, but nonetheless, these lies have become part of his persona.

In 1875, Poe's remains were reinterred with those of Maria Clemm at the Poe Memorial Gravesite, located near the corner of Fayette and Greene Streets in Baltimore, Maryland. A bust of Poe adorns the marble and granite monument, which is simply inscribed with the

Edgar Allan Poe's original gravesite at the Old Westminster Burying Ground of Baltimore.

birth and death dates of Poe (although his birth date is wrong). At the dedication ceremony, letters were read from Henry Wadsworth Longfellow and Alfred Lord Tennyson, with Walt Whitman in attendance. On Poe's original gravesite now stands a stone carving of a raven with the inscription: "Quoth the Raven, Nevermore." Beginning in 1949, a mysterious fan began making pilgrimages to Poe's grave, known as "The Poe Toaster." The tradition was carried on for more than sixty years, and it is likely that "The Poe Toaster" was actually several individuals. Tradition holds that in the early morning hours of the anniversary of Poe's birthdate, January 19th, this unknown mourner arrived at Poe's grave and raised a glass of cognac in tribute to the poet, leaving behind three roses. Members of the Edgar Allan Poe Society in Baltimore have helped protect this tradition for decades. On August 15, 2007, Sam Porpora, a former historian at the Westminster Church in Baltimore, claimed that he had started the tradition as a hoax to raise money and enhance the profile of the church. His story has never been confirmed, but the last documented appearance of "The Poe Toaster" was on January 19, 2009, the bicentennial of Poe's birth.

Edgar Allan Poe was reinterred at this gravesite in 1875 at the Old Westminster Burying Ground of Baltimore.

> *"I find the great thing in this world is not so much where we stand, as in what direction we are moving — we must sail sometimes with the wind and sometimes against it - but we must sail, and not drift, nor lie at anchor."*
>
> OLIVER WENDELL HOLMES SR.

Oliver Wendell Holmes Sr. *Courtesy of the Library of Congress, Prints & Photographs Division, George G. Bain Collection, LC-DIG-GGBAIN-03800.*

POET, SHORT STORY WRITER & ESSAYIST

Born: Cambridge, Massachusetts

Died: Boston, Massachusetts

Buried: Mount Auburn Cemetery
Cambridge, Massachusetts

Oliver Wendell Holmes Sr. was a man of diverse talents. He was both a celebrated physician and professor at Harvard University and an accomplished author who published countless essays and short stories on various subjects. He was also one of the founding editors of *The Atlantic Monthly*. He was born on August 29, 1809, in Cambridge, Massachusetts, the son of Reverend Abiel Holmes and Sarah Wendell. They lived in the "Old Gambrel-roofed House" in the Harvard College-dominated village, which he later memorialized in *The Autocrat of the Breakfast Table* (1858).

As a young child, Holmes was considered small for his age and suffered from numerous health issues, including asthma. He was known for his precocious nature and, although he excelled at academics, he was often criticized for his lack of participation and tendency to read during lectures. He was enrolled at the Port School, a private academy near Cambridge, Massachusetts, where one of his classmates was future critic and author Margaret Fuller.

Holmes was raised in a very strict Calvinist household and his father wanted him to pursue a career in theology. In 1824, he was sent to Phillips Academy in Andover, Maryland. Holmes' father sent him there because of the school's Calvinist ideology, but Oliver had no intention of following in his father's footsteps. After only one year at Phillips Academy, Holmes decided to transfer to Harvard. During his days at Harvard, Holmes' interests were wide and varied. During this period, he wrote many poems, a few of which were published in the *Harvard Collegian*. He graduated in 1829, after which he briefly studied law before turning his attention to medicine. In 1830, he wrote one of his most famous poems, the patriotic "Old Ironsides," which was published in the *Boston Daily Advertiser*. This poem helped to save the Navy frigate USS *Constitution* from being dismantled and earned Holmes national recognition. After spending several years studying medicine at the most celebrated medical schools in Paris, Holmes returned to Harvard and received his medical degree in 1836. He swiftly distinguished himself within medical circles by writing articles and essays on a variety of medical issues and reforms, most conspicuously the treatment for malaria. During this same period, he also continued his literary pursuits and, in 1836, published a collection of poetry entitled *Poems*. In 1838, he was appointed a Professor of Anatomy at Dartmouth College, but two years later returned to Harvard.

Holmes married Amelia Lee Jackson in Boston, Massachusetts, on June 15, 1840. She was the daughter of Massachusetts Supreme Court Justice Charles Jackson. They would have three children, one of whom, Oliver Wendell Holmes Jr., would become an Associate Justice of the U.S. Supreme Court. The younger Holmes would fight for the Union in the American Civil War, and, in 1862, his father wrote *My Hunt after the Captain*, which was published in *The Atlantic Monthly*. It was a retelling of his search for his son who had been wounded at the Battle of Antietam. Holmes Jr. accused his father of using his ordeal for literary gain and this would cause great strain in their relationship.

In the ensuing years, Holmes became a sought-after lecturer. He also published a number of noteworthy medical studies, including *The Contagiousness of Puerperal Fever* (1843) published in a number of journals including the *Boston Medical and Surgical Journal* and in the *North American Review*. In the controversial study, Holmes argued that the cause of puerperal fever, a deadly infection contracted by women after childbirth, was caused by patient-to-patient contact via their physicians. Holmes concluded that any physician whose patient had contacted puerperal fever had the ethical obligation to first purify all medical instruments and

Oliver Wendell Holmes Jr., Associate Justice of the U.S. Supreme Court (1902-1932) and son of famed writer Oliver Wendell Holmes Sr. *Courtesy of the Library of Congress, Prints & Photographs Division, LC-F81-33175.*

then discontinue their obstetric medical practices for a period of at least six months. Holmes is also credited with coining the word "anesthesia." In an 1846 letter to dentist William Morton, Holmes wrote: "Everybody wants to have a hand in a great discovery. All I will do is to give a hint or two as to names, or the name to be applied to the state produced and the agent. The state should, I think, be called 'Anesthesia.' This signifies insensibility, more particularly...to objects of touch."

Holmes was appointed Professor of Anatomy and Physiology at Harvard Medical School in 1847, a position he would hold for another thirty-four years. He would also serve as the Dean of the department from 1847 to 1853. Medical training in Paris led Holmes to teach his students the importance of anatomical pathology in the diagnosis of disease.

DID YOU KNOW?

Oliver Wendell Holmes invented the American stereoscope, a 19th century entertainment device in which pictures were viewed in 3-D. He later wrote an explanation for its popularity, stating: "There was not any wholly new principle involved in its construction, but, it proved so much more convenient than any hand-instrument in use." Rather than patenting the hand stereopticon and profiting from its success, Holmes gave the idea away.

Between 1851 and 1856, Holmes lectured throughout New England. He spoke about a variety of subjects that ranged from medicine to English poets of the 19th century. As social attitudes began to change, however, Holmes often found himself publicly at odds with those he called moral bullies. Because of mounting criticism from the press regarding his vocal anti-abolitionism, as well as his dislike of the growing temperance movement, he chose to discontinue his lecturing and return home.

Gravesite of Oliver Wendell Holmes Sr. at Mount Auburn Cemetery in Cambridge, Massachusetts.

In 1856, *The Atlantic Monthly* was launched. This new magazine contained articles and essays from many of the leading literary figures of the period. For the first issue, Holmes wrote a new version of an earlier essay, "The Autocrat at the Breakfast-Table." The critical acclaim of this essay helped secure the initial success of the journal. In 1858, this essay was turned into a book and published under the same title. A sequel, *The Professor at the Breakfast-Table*, was published the following year, and these two works have become some of Holmes' most enduring works.

In 1861, Holmes published his first novel, *Elsie Venner: a Romance of Destiny*. In the book, he explored the theme of original sin and gracefully captured the spirit of small-town America. The novel was originally serialized in *The Atlantic Monthly* and it initially drew a wide range of criticism. In the coming years, Holmes' literary fame continued to grow and he published numerous essays, poems, and books, including *Songs in Many Keys* (1862), *Soundings from the Atlantic* (1864), *The Guardian Angel* (1867), *The Poet at the Breakfast-Table* (1872), *Songs of Many Seasons* (1875), and *The Iron Gate and Other Poems* (1880). In 1884, he published a book dedicated to the life and works of his friend, Ralph Waldo Emerson. Later biographers would use this book as an outline for their own studies. The section dedicated to Emerson's poetry, into which Holmes had particular insight, proved particularly useful. Beginning in January 1885, his third and final novel, *A Mortal Antipathy*, was serially published in *The Atlantic Monthly*. The following year, Holmes and his daughter, Amelia, embarked on a tour of Europe with a busy itinerary of socializing with various associates and friends. His memoir, *Our Hundred Days in Europe* (1887), is a recounting of this trip.

Towards the end of his life, Holmes became bitter and depressed. He often dwelled upon the fact that he had outlived his wife, most of his friends, and literary contemporaries, such as Emerson, Longfellow, Lowell, and Hawthorne. As he said, "I feel like my own survivor...We were on deck together as we began the voyage of life...Then the craft which held us began going to pieces." Holmes made his last public appearance at a reception for the National Education Association in Boston on February 23, 1893, where he read the poem "To the Teachers of America." On Sunday afternoon, October 7, 1894, Holmes died quietly in his sleep at his home in Boston, Massachusetts. His son, Oliver Wendell Holmes Jr., wrote: "His death was as peaceful as one could wish for those one loves, he simply ceased to breathe." Holmes' memorial service was held at King's Chapel in Boston and he was buried beside his wife, Amelia (who had died on February 6, 1888), at Mount Auburn Cemetery in Cambridge, Massachusetts.

Harriet Beecher Stowe
(1811-1896)

Harriet Beecher Stowe, photograph circa 1880. *Courtesy of the Library of Congress, Prints & Photographs Division, LC-USZ62-11212.*

NOVELIST

Born: Litchfield, Connecticut

Died: Hartford, Connecticut

Buried: Phillips Academy Cemetery

Andover, Massachusetts

"Did not write it. God wrote it. I merely did His dictation."

HARRIET BEECHER STOWE

Harriet Beecher Stowe's literary works were a product of the culture of her time and represent a crusading sense of social and political accountability. The far-reaching impact of her novel, *Uncle Tom's Cabin*, made Stowe one of the most widely celebrated American writers of the mid-19th century. Harriet Elizabeth Beecher was born on June 14, 1811, in Litchfield, Connecticut, the daughter of Lyman Beecher, a well-known evangelical Calvinist preacher, and Roxana Foote. Her father's strict religious ideology paved the way for Harriett and her siblings to walk the straight and narrow path of devotion to God, and to himself. Her father's religious influence would play a significant role in Harriet's later writings.

Reverend Lyman Beecher, circa 1855-1865. *Courtesy of the Library of Congress, Prints & Photographs Division, LC-BH82-5113B.*

The Harriett Beecher Stowe House in Cincinnati, Ohio. Located on the former campus of the Lane Seminary, Harriet Beecher Stowe lived here until her marriage in 1836.

The Harriet Beecher Stowe House in Brunswick, Maine. The author lived here when she wrote *Uncle Tom's Cabin*. Her husband was teaching theology at nearby Bowdoin College, and she regularly invited friends from the college to read and discuss the chapters before publication.

The Beecher family moved to Cincinnati, Ohio, in 1832, when Reverend Beecher was appointed administrator of the Lane Theological Seminary. It was here that his oldest child, Catherine, opened the Western Female Institute, a school where Harriet would later teach. It was during this period that Harriet began to write. In 1834, she won a prize for her story "A New England Sketch," which was published in *Western Monthly Magazine*. She began writing regular articles for the magazine and other popular periodicals, like *The Atlantic Monthly*.

On January 6, 1836, she married Calvin Ellis Stowe, a professor at the Lane Seminary. Together they would have seven children. During this period, Lane Seminary became one of the epicenters of extreme abolitionism, but Harriet initially did not agree with these radical principles. Only after visiting the South and observing slavery in action did her thinking begin to change.

In 1849, she published her first novel, *The Mayflower*. The following year, Calvin Stowe was asked to teach theology at Bowdoin College in Brunswick, Maine. It was during this period (1851-1852) that Harriet began to write her most famous novel, *Uncle Tom's Cabin*, which was serialized in *The National Era*, a Washington, D.C. anti-slavery newspaper. The book was published in a two-volume print edition in 1852 and was a huge success, selling half a million copies in five years. Although *Uncle Tom's Cabin* was well received in the North, its reception was almost completely opposite in the southern states. The book details the life of Tom, a slave, as he passed through the hands of three different owners, each of whom is meant to represent a different type of Southern figure. The first is a kind farmer, the second a Southern gentleman, and the third, the immoral Simon Legree. The fortunes of the slaves in the book spiral downward until the very end, when two of them escaped to freedom. The overall treatment of the slave and master relationship in the book exposed something far more complex than abolitionist ideas.

Following the success of *Uncle Tom's Cabin*, Stowe began to lecture and traveled extensively, receiving praise throughout Europe. She answered her critics by writing *A Key to Uncle Tom's Cabin* (1853), a book designed to document the facts behind the subjects of her earlier novel. In 1856, she published another novel, *Dred: A Tale of the Great Dismal Swamp*, but it was not well-received and did not come close to equaling the societal impact or financial success of *Uncle Tom's Cabin*. Her literary reputation for years to come was connected with the instructional power of her first two novels, but she soon abandoned the topic of slavery in favor of instructive writings, producing a series of works based on the New England lifestyle. In 1869, Stowe traveled to Europe, where she renewed an earlier friendship with Lord Byron's widow. As a result, Stowe wrote *Lady Byron Vindicated* (1870). In the sensationalized book, she alleged that Byron had violated his marriage vows by having a sexual relationship with his sister. Byron was already a living literary legend by this time and Stowe's reputation suffered greatly after writing this titillating book. Undaunted by this setback, she continued to write novels, poems, and her autobiography.

Reverend Henry Ward Beecher, circa 1855-1865. *Courtesy of the Library of Congress, Prints & Photographs Division, LC-BH82-4555C.*

In early 1870, Henry Ward Beecher, Harriet's younger brother, a well-known social reformer and clergyman, was accused of adultery and became the subject of a national scandal. Unable to stand the public ridicule of her brother, Stowe traveled to Florida, asking family members to keep her informed of the proceedings. Throughout the scandal, Stowe remained loyal to her brother and believed he was innocent of the accusations. Beecher was eventually exonerated of the charges in 1875. In the last years of her life, Stowe tried to manage her literary income with limited success and, following the death of her husband in 1887, she became severely depressed. On July 1, 1896, Harriet Beecher Stowe died from natural causes at her home in Hartford, Connecticut, and was buried beside her husband at the Phillips Academy Cemetery in Andover, Massachusetts.

The Harriet Beecher Stowe House in Hartford, Connecticut. The author lived in this home for the last twenty-three years of her life and died here on July 1, 1896. The house is adjacent to that of fellow author Mark Twain.

Gravesite of Harriet Beecher Stowe at the historic cemetery at Phillips Academy in Andover, Massachusetts.

"Go confidently in the direction of your dreams. Live the life you have imagined."

HENRY DAVID THOREAU

Henry David Thoreau was a man of simple tastes who was known for his keen sense of observation. His writings on government were considered revolutionary, with some calling him an early anarchist. Because of his essays on nature, he is often called the "father of environmentalism." While the works of many of his contemporaries have faded into obscurity, Thoreau's essays have endured the test of time because of their relevancy in today's world.

He was born on July 12, 1817, in Concord, Massachusetts, the son of John Thoreau and Cynthia Dunbar. As a young boy, he excelled at academics and was eventually admitted to Harvard College, where he studied classic languages. After graduating from college in 1837, Thoreau struggled with what to do next. At the time, an educated man like Thoreau might have chosen to pursue a career in law, medicine, theology, or education. In 1838, he established a school with his brother, John. The school closed a few years later, after his brother became ill; Thoreau then went to work at his father's pencil factory in Concord.

The Thoreau farm in Concord, Massachusetts. Henry David Thoreau was born here on July 12, 1817.

It was during this time that he befriended Ralph Waldo Emerson, through whom he became aware of the ideology of Transcendentalism, a school of thought that emphasized the importance of practical thinking and encouraged scientific examination and observation. Thoreau came to know many of the movement's leading figures, including Bronson Alcott and Margaret Fuller. Emerson acted as a mentor to Thoreau and supported his early literary efforts, which were first published in *The Dial*, a Transcendentalist magazine. Emerson also gave Thoreau access to his property at Walden Pond, which would inspire one of his greatest works.

Henry David Thoreau
(1817-1862)

Henry David Thoreau from an undated photograph. *Courtesy of the Library of Congress, Prints & Photographs Division, LC-USZ61-361.*

POET & ESSAYIST

Born: Concord, Massachusetts

Died: Concord, Massachusetts

Buried: Sleepy Hollow Cemetery
Concord, Massachusetts

Replica of Henry David Thoreau's cabin at Walden Pond.

In 1845, Thoreau began living on Walden Pond, where he started to write the classic *Walden, or, Life in the Woods* (1854). He built a small cabin on Emerson's property, where he spent more than two years searching for a simpler lifestyle. During his time at Walden, Thoreau experimented with working as little as possible and rebelled against the accepted norms of society; he felt "the mass of men lead lives of quiet desperation." He also felt that this avant-garde philosophy helped him avoid the melancholy that was common in society. Thoreau's time at Walden Pond gave him plenty of time to ponder philosophy and write. It was during this time that he wrote *A Week on the Concord and Merrimack Rivers* (1849), which drew from a boating trip he took with his brother in 1839. The public's interest in his strange new lifestyle provided Thoreau with the creative spark to write a collection of his famous Walden essays. The collection at first received mixed reviews, but was a modest financial success, and since its publication, has inspired legions of loyal naturalists, environmentalists, and writers.

In late July 1846, an incident would occur that would inspire Thoreau to write another of his most famous essays. Legend states that while living at Walden Pond, Thoreau encountered a local tax collector who asked him to pay six years' delinquent poll taxes. Thoreau refused to pay the taxes because of his opposition to the Mexican American War and slavery. Because of this, Thoreau was arrested and spent one night in jail. This experience had a huge impact on Thoreau and, from January to February 1848, he delivered a series of lectures in Concord on "The Rights and Duties of the Individual in Relation to Government," in which he explained why he was opposed to paying taxes. These lectures would later become the essay "Civil Disobedience," which was published in May 1849 by Elizabeth Peabody in the *Aesthetic Papers*. In this essay, Thoreau made a strong case for acting on personal conscience and not blindly following laws and governmental policy. He wrote "the only obligation which I have a right to assume is to do at any time what I think right." Since its publication in 1849, "Civil Disobedience" has inspired numerous protest movements around the world.

On September 6, 1847, Thoreau left Walden Pond and moved back to Concord to manage Emerson's household while he traveled to Europe. Always fascinated with nature, Thoreau traveled throughout New England, often visiting the woods of Maine, the shores of Cape Cod, and other locations. He remained a devoted abolitionist until the end of his life. To support this cause, he wrote several essays, including "Slavery in Massachusetts" (1854). He also took a courageous stand for John Brown, a radical abolitionist who led a failed uprising against slavery. Brown and his supporters raided a federal arsenal at Harpers Ferry, Virginia, on October 16, 1859, but the raid was thwarted and Brown was later convicted of treason and executed. Thoreau defended Brown's ideals and actions with the speech "A Plea for Capt. John Brown."

Though Thoreau was romantically involved with several women during his lifetime, most notably Ellen Seawall and Mary Russell, he never married. In his later years, he battled numerous illnesses, including tuberculosis. His health steadily declined with brief periods of

remission until he became bedridden. He spent his last years revising and editing works, such as *The Maine Woods and Excursions*, which was posthumously published in 1864. Friends were fascinated by his peaceful acceptance of his imminent death. Thoreau died on May 6, 1862, in Concord and his last words were alleged to be, "now comes good sailing," followed by two lone words, "moose" and "Indian." Bronson Alcott planned his funeral service and read selections from Thoreau's works, Ellery Channing presented a hymn, and Ralph Waldo Emerson wrote the eulogy. Thoreau was originally buried within the Dunbar family plot at Sleepy Hollow Cemetery in Concord. His remains, along with other members of his immediate family, were eventually reinterred on "Authors Ridge" within the same cemetery.

Gravesite of Henry David Thoreau on Author's Ridge at Sleepy Hollow Cemetery in Concord, Massachusetts.

Herman Melville
(1819 - 1891)

Herman Melville from an undated photograph.

NOVELIST, SHORT STORY WRITER, ESSAYIST & POET

Born: New York City, New York

Died: New York City, New York

Buried: Woodlawn Cemetery, The Bronx, New York

"It is better to fail in originality than to succeed in imitation."

HERMAN MELVILLE

Herman Melville's literary career was one of great success and tremendous lows. His first three novels were well-received, but after these initial literary successes, his popularity quickly declined and was never recovered during his lifetime. By the time of his death, in 1891, he was almost completely forgotten. It was not until the early 20th century that his works won renewed recognition, especially *Moby Dick*, which was hailed as one of the masterpieces of both American and world literature.

He was born on August 1, 1819, in New York City, the child of Allan Melvill and Maria Gansevort. The family surname was changed to Melville in 1834, after the death of his father. Part of an illustrious Boston family, Herman's father traveled extensively as a commission agent and merchant. His paternal grandfather, Major Thomas Mevill, was a participant in the Boston Tea Party and a radical who steadfastly refused to adapt to the times. He was immortalized in Oliver Wendell Holmes' poem "The Last Leaf." As a child, Herman did not fit into conventional molds and, as a result, his parents were quite disappointed in him. In 1826, Allan Melvill wrote that his son was "backward in speech and somewhat slow in comprehension, but of a docile and amiable disposition."

In 1830, financially overextended and psychologically unbalanced, Herman's father moved the family to Albany and began a fur business. The new enterprise was disastrous and he was forced to declare bankruptcy. He died soon afterward, leaving the family destitute. By this time, Herman had already begun to write, but continued financial problems for the family forced him to focus primarily on non-literary ventures. His nomadic nature and a prevailing longing to gain financial autonomy led him to seek employment as a surveyor on the Erie Canal. This effort was unsuccessful, and his brother helped him secure a job as a cabin boy on a ship bound for Liverpool. Although he appeared to enjoy this nautical way of life, Melville did not devote himself to the sea. His novel, *Redburn: His First Voyage* (1849), was partially based on this first ocean passage.

Between 1837 and 1840, Melville taught school in Lansingburgh, New York, but by late 1840, he once again turned to the sea for employment. He set sail aboard the whaler *Acushnet* on January 3, 1841, bound for the South Pacific. He would later remark that his life began that day, but he left no account of the events of this eighteen-month journey. In July of 1842, while in the Marquesas Islands, Melville abandoned the ship, and for several weeks lived among the native islanders. He would later write about these adventures in his first novel, *Typee: A Peep at Polynesian Life* (1846). Melville was not overly worried about the consequences of abandoning the *Acushnet* and soon found employment aboard another whaler, the *Lucy Ann*, which was bound for Tahiti. During this brief period, he took part in an ill-fated mutiny and was briefly imprisoned. Following his release, Melville spent several months drifting aimlessly across the nearby islands and eventually agreed to sign on with another whaling vessel. His whaling adventures came to an end in April 1843 in Hawaii, where he became a passionate opponent of the activities of the Christian missionaries. After a few months, he joined the crew of the USS *United States*, and arrived back in Boston in October 1844.

When Melville returned to the United States, he found that his family's financial affairs had greatly improved. His brother, Gansevoort, was attaining political renown and had been appointed secretary at the embassy in London by President James K. Polk. With his family's encouragement, Melville began to write about his adventures of the South Seas. What resulted were the novels *Typee: A Peep at Polynesian Life* (1846) and *Omoo: A Narrative of Adventures in the South Seas* (1847). Both books were bestsellers and were received well by critics. On August 4, 1847, he married Elizabeth Shaw, the daughter of Lemuel Shaw, Chief Justice of the Massachusetts Supreme Court. They moved to New York City, where he wrote most of *Mardi* (1849), completed *Redburn* (1849) and *White-Jacket* (1850), and began the first chapters of *Moby Dick*.

"Arrowhead," the home of Herman Melville from 1847–1860 in Pittsfield, Massachusetts.

In 1850, Melville purchased "Arrowhead," a farm house in Pittsfield, Massachusetts, where he lived for thirteen years and continued to write. While living at Arrowhead, he befriended Nathaniel Hawthorne, who lived in nearby Lenox. This relationship reanimated Melville's creativity, and though the two men would gradually grow apart, their time as neighbors in 1850 helped shape what would become one of the greatest works of American literature. Melville promised his publisher that *Moby Dick* would be completed by the fall of 1850. The novel tells the story of an itinerant sailor named Ishmael and his voyage aboard the whaler *Pequod* commanded by Captain Ahab. Ishmael soon becomes aware of Ahab's intentions: to seek out Moby Dick, a mysterious white sperm whale. In an earlier encounter, the whale had sunk Ahab's ship and bit off his leg. The legacy of this ill-fated event haunts Ahab, who is bent on seeking revenge. In *Moby Dick*, Melville successfully used symbolism and metaphor to convey the intricate themes of the novel. The novel was published in October 1851 in London and a month later in America, but was not well-received.

In the aftermath of *Moby Dick's* failure, Melville became more and more reclusive, and friends feared for his sanity. He soon began to write *Pierre* (1852), which was yet another critical and financial disaster. Only 33 years old, Melville saw his literary career in ruins. His publisher rejected his next manuscript, which weighed heavily on his mind. Nearing a complete mental collapse after facing the disaster of a fire at his New York publisher's property that destroyed the original manuscripts of all his books, Melville began to write *Israel Potter* (1855). The book had modest financial and critical success, which led Melville to contribute several short stories to *Putnam's Monthly Magazine*. These tales reflected Melville's growing despondency and disdain for human hypocrisy and greed. In late 1856, he traveled to England and spent several days visiting his old friend Nathaniel Hawthorne. At the seaside resort village of Southport, Hawthorne made his now-famous evaluation of Melville in a journal entry dated November 20, 1856:

Gravesite of Herman Melville and his wife at Woodlawn Cemetery, The Bronx, New York.

Melville, as he always does, began to reason of Providence and futurity, and of everything that lies beyond human ken, and informed me that he "pretty much made up his mind to be annihilated": but still he does not seem to rest in that anticipation; and, I think, will never rest until he gets hold of a definite belief. It is strange how he persists and has persisted ever since I knew him, and probably long before in wandering to and fro over these deserts, as dismal and monotonous as the sand hills amid which we were sitting. He can neither believe, nor be comfortable in his unbelief; and he is too honest and courageous not to try to do one or the other. If he were a religious man, he would be one of the most truly religious and reverential; he has a very high and noble nature, and better worth immortality than most of us.

In 1857, Melville published *The Confidence-Man*, which was the last novel published in his lifetime. The novel is a depressing satire that concentrates on American corruption and broken dreams. By the early 1860s, with a large family to support, Melville actively sought out a political post, but did not receive an appointment. When the Civil War broke out, he volunteered for the Navy, but was again rejected. That same year, he received a bit of financial assistance when his wife inherited a modest sum after her father's death. The carnage and human toll of the war greatly affected him and furnished the subject matter for his first volume of poetry, *Battle Pieces and Aspects of the War* (1866). Several months after its publication, Melville was appointed customs inspector on the New York docks, which finally brought a stable income.

In the coming years, several heartbreaking misfortunes descended upon the Melville family. First, his son, Malcolm, accidently shot himself after a quarrel with his father. Then in 1886, Melville's second son, Stanwix, died in a San Francisco hospital after a long illness. Throughout these painful events, and for the whole of his nineteen years working at the customs house, Melville's literary output was practically non-existent. By the time his second collection of poetry, *John Marr, and Other Sailors; With Some Sea-Pieces*, was published in 1888, he had been retired for three years. In 1891, he wrote his final collection of poems, *Timoleon* (1891), and then returned to novels, which culminated in his last work, *Billy Budd* (which remained unpublished until 1924). On the morning of September 28, 1891, Melville died from a heart attack at his home in New York City and was buried at Woodlawn Cemetery in The Bronx, New York.

Walt Whitman
(1819–1892)

The "Quaker photo" of Walt Whitman (1870). *Courtesy of the Library of Congress, Prints & Photographs Division, LC-USZ62-82781.*

POET, NOVELIST & ESSAYIST

Born: West Hills, Long Island, New York

Died: Camden, New Jersey

Buried: Harleigh Cemetery, Camden, New Jersey

Walt Whitman is considered by many to be the first true poet of American democracy. The title was intended to reflect upon his knack for writing in a uniquely American style. The poets of the Beat Generation of the 1950s and 1960s often emulated his drifter lifestyle. During his lifetime, Whitman was an outspoken supporter of temperance and an intermittent advocate of prohibition. He once claimed that he didn't taste "strong liquor" until he was thirty. Whitman was profoundly influenced by the philosophy of deism, the basic ideology of which is reason and examination of the natural world, without the need for structured religion, can confirm that life is the product of a creator. He embraced all religions in the same way, and denied that any one conviction was more important than another. His poetry depicted love and sexuality in a plain and distinctive manner that was not familiar to American culture in the 19th century. Because of this, his sexual orientation has been questioned. It is generally believed that Whitman was homosexual or bisexual based on his poetry, though it is uncertain and disputed.

Walter Whitman Jr. was born on May 31, 1819, in West Hills, Long Island, New York, to Walter Whitman Sr. and Louisa Van Velsor. The Whitman family was forced to move from West Hills to Brooklyn in 1823 due to financial difficulties. Because of his parents' financial problems, Whitman would later reflect on his childhood as being unsettling and generally discontented. At age 11, he finished formal schooling and sought out various employment opportunities, including an apprenticeship in a printing office.

By 1841, Whitman was living in New York City, where he began to write. Many of his short stories and poems of this time period were imitations of other popular works, as was his first novel, *Franklin Evans, or The Inebriate* (1842). Whitman continued to write and edit articles for several newspapers and magazines over the next few years. In 1848, he was fired from the *Brooklyn Eagle* because of his political opinions. He then traveled south, where he temporarily worked for the *New Orleans Crescent*. Very little is known of Whitman's life during this time, which might account for his rapid transformation from journalist to activist poet.

41

In Whitman's first edition of *Leaves of Grass* (1855), the work opens with a rather casual portrait of the author, who styled himself as "poet of the people," and was dressed in casual work clothes. In the drawn-out preface, Whitman announced that his poetry would celebrate the greatness of the new nation: "The Americans of all nations at any time upon the earth have probably the fullest poetical nature. The United States themselves are essentially the greatest poem," and of its peoples: "The largeness of nature or the nation were monstrous without a corresponding largeness and generosity of the spirit of the citizen." In the first edition of the work, Whitman turned away from the customary writing styles of the past and instead relied upon the rhythms of common dialects, and especially delighted in the use of informal and slang terminology.

Unfortunately, the first edition of *Leaves of Grass* sold poorly, but luckily Whitman had sent Ralph Waldo Emerson a free copy and, in his now-famous reply, Emerson wrote: "I find it the most extraordinary piece of wit and wisdom that America has yet contributed...I greet you at the beginning of a great career." Emerson's letter had a deep impact on Whitman, completely overriding the otherwise meager reaction the work had received. For the second edition of *Leaves of Grass* (1856), Whitman added twenty new poems to his original twelve. With this version, he would begin a lifelong practice of adding and deleting poems to new editions of the work. He would revise previously published versions in order to bring the work into line with his present moods and mindset. The third edition of *Leaves of Grass* (1860) was purchased by a Boston publisher, one of the few times in Whitman's writing career that he did not have to self-publish. This version, which Whitman referred to as his "new Bible," contained all of the earlier poems, plus one hundred forty-six new ones. Whitman arranged many of the poems in special groupings, a practice he continued in all later editions.

During the Civil War, Whitman traveled to Virginia in search of his brother, George, who had been reported as wounded in action. He remained in Washington, D.C., devoting many hours as a volunteer nurse at local hospitals and attending to the needs of wounded soldiers. His daily interaction with the horrors of wounded soldiers and death had a profound effect on his mental and physical health. The impact of these experiences was reflected in *Drum-Taps* (1865). In this collection of poems, Whitman was able to express through dignified simplicity the shock, isolation, and suffering that was caused by the conflict. In the coming years, his poetry began to center on themes, such as the soul, death, and the existence of life after death. Within a dozen years, Whitman reinvented himself as a celestial poet of global understanding. Such poems as "Whispers of Heavenly Death," "Darest Thou Now O Soul," "The Last Invocation," and "A Noiseless Patient Spider," with their emphasis on spirituality, paved the way for "Passage to India" (1871), Whitman's most important and ambitious poem of the post-Civil War era.

In early 1873, Whitman suffered a stroke and was forced to live with his brother in Camden, New Jersey. During this same period, his mother died. These events left him severely depressed. Even though he was slowed and nearly bedridden by the effects of the stroke, Whitman still found time to edit several editions of *Leaves of Grass*. In 1891, Whitman commissioned the building of a granite mausoleum at Harleigh Cemetery and visited it often during construction. In the last week of his life, he wrote: "I suffer all the time: I have no relief, no escape: it is monotony, monotony, monotony, in pain." Walt Whitman died on March 26, 1892, at his home in Camden, New Jersey. An autopsy revealed his lungs had diminished to one-eighth of their normal breathing capability, a result of bronchial pneumonia, and that a large abscess tumor on his chest had destroyed one of his ribs. A public memorial was held at his Camden home, where more than a thousand mourners paid their last respects. Whitman's oak coffin was barely visible through the floral arrangements. Four days after his death, he was buried within his tomb at Harleigh Cemetery in Camden, New Jersey.

1– The Walt Whitman House in Camden, New Jersey, where he spent the last years of his life and died on March 26, 1892.

2– Walt Whitman's tomb at Harleigh Cemetery in Camden, New Jersey.

Emily Dickinson
(1830–1886)

Daguerreotype of Emily Dickinson, taken circa 1848. *Courtesy of the Yale University Manuscripts & Archives Digital Images Database, Yale University, Todd-Bingham Picture Collection and Family Papers.*

POET

Born: Amherst, Massachusetts

Died: Amherst, Massachusetts

Buried: Amherst West Cemetery, Amherst, Massachusetts

"If I read a book and it makes my whole body so cold no fire can ever warm me, I know that is poetry."

EMILY DICKINSON

Emily Dickinson lived a mostly introverted and reclusive life. She had a peculiar fondness for wearing only white clothing and, later in life, rarely left her room. Most of her friendships were carried out through correspondence. Fewer than a dozen of her nearly 1,800 poems were published during her lifetime. She questioned the puritanical beliefs of Calvinism and poignantly explored her own spirituality, through emotional and deeply personal poetry. Her poems were unique and often contained short lines, lacked titles, and used avant-garde grammar and punctuation. Many of her poems dealt with the themes of death and immortality.

She was born on December 10, 1830, in Amherst, Massachusetts, the daughter of Edward Dickinson, a successful lawyer and congressman, and Emily Norcross. Her grandfather, Samuel Fowler Dickinson, was one of the founders of Amherst College. The Dickinsons were staunch advocates of education and Emily benefited from an exceptional education. At the age of seventeen, she left home to attend the Mount Holyoke Female Seminary. She returned home less than a year later, suffering from severe homesickness and poor health. She then began to write and spent more and more time alone.

The Emily Dickinson "Homestead" in Amherst, Massachusetts, where the poet was born on December 10, 1830 and died May 15, 1886.

The Dickinson "Homestead" was expanded in 1855 to include gardens and a conservatory. Amherst College's commencement reception was held at the home. The following year, Emily's brother, William, a successful lawyer and Harvard graduate, married Emily's best friend, Susan Gilbert. The couple moved into their home, "The Evergreens," a wedding gift, where they often entertained such guests as Ralph Waldo Emerson and Samuel Bowles, editor of *The Springfield Republican*. The latter would publish some of Emily's poems in his newspaper and became a love interest.

By the early 1860s, Emily started to avoid social activities, but also began a period of very prolific writing. Modern literary scholars are divided as to the cause for Dickinson's social anxiety. While she was diagnosed as having a nervous disorder by her doctor, some believe she may have suffered from illnesses as varied as agoraphobia (a disorder characterized by anxiety in public places) and possibly epilepsy. In 1862, the *Atlantic Monthly* sent out a public call for poetry submissions, and Emily sent some of her work. She soon became friends with the *Atlantic's* chief editor, Thomas Wentworth Higginson. The two exchanged many letters and it has been speculated that Emily had more than platonic feelings for him.

In the coming years, Dickinson rarely left her home, and as early as 1867, she began speaking to visitors through her bedroom door rather than face-to-face. The few people she exchanged letters with during her last fifteen years of life never saw her in person. The Dickinson family became very protective of Emily's privacy and decided that her behavior was not to be discussed with strangers. Around the time of her father's death in 1874, Emily stopped going out in public, but continued to maintain friendships by writing letters.

In the last years of her life, Emily stopped editing and organizing her poems. She also forced her sister, Lavinia, to promise to destroy her papers upon her death. On June 16, 1874, Emily's father, Edward Dickinson, suffered a stroke and died. When his funeral was held at the Dickinson home, Emily stayed in her room with the door cracked open. A year later, on June 15, 1875, Emily's mother suffered a stroke and was rendered an invalid. These and other events had a profound effect on Emily, and in the fall of 1884, she wrote that "the dyings (sic) have been too deep for me, and before I could raise my heart from one, another has come." Earlier in the year, she had suffered a fainting spell and was confined to her bed, but managed to send a final burst of letters in the spring. What is thought to be her last letter was sent to her cousins, Louise and Frances Norcross, and simply read: "Little Cousins, Called Back. Emily."

On May 15, 1886, Emily Dickinson died at her home. Her brother wrote in his diary that "the day was awful...she ceased to breathe that terrible breathing just before the (afternoon) whistle sounded for six." Her doctor recorded the cause of death as Bright's disease and listed the duration of her illness as two-and-a-half years. She was buried in a white coffin, wearing one of her favorite white dresses. At the funeral service, held in the Dickinsons' home, Unitarian minister and author Thomas Wentworth Higginson, who had met Emily only

Close-up view of Emily Dickinson's grave marker.

The Dickinson family burial plot at Amherst West Cemetery. Emily Dickinson's grave marker is located in the center.

twice, read "No Coward Soul Is Mine," a poem by Emily Bronte that had been a favorite of Dickinson's. Her coffin was then carried through fields of buttercups for burial in the family plot at Amherst West Cemetery.

After her death, Lavinia kept her promise to destroy Emily's papers. Ironically, she had left no instructions about miscellaneous notebooks and other papers found locked in a chest. Lavinia recognized the worth of these writings and sought to have them published. A family feud ensued that ended with the manuscripts being divided among numerous relatives. This prevented complete publication of Dickinson's poetry for many years. The first volume of her poems, edited jointly by Mabel Loomis Todd and Thomas Wentworth Higginson, was published in November 1890. This 115-poem collection was a critical and financial success. In 1891, *Poems: Second Series* was published, which included nearly a dozen poems. Other editions of previously unpublished or newly edited works were published between 1914 and 1945. Martha Dickinson Bianchi, the daughter of Susan and Edward Dickinson, published editions of her aunt's poetry based on the manuscripts held by her side of the family, whereas Mabel Loomis Todd's daughter, Millicent Todd Bingham, published works based on the manuscripts held by her mother. These competing collections of poetry ensured that the poet's work was in continuous print.

"Good books, like good friends, are few and chosen; the more select, the more enjoyable."

LOUISA MAY ALCOTT

Louisa May Alcott, circa 1880.

Louisa May Alcott was born on November 29, 1832, in Germantown, Pennsylvania, the daughter of Amos Bronson Alcott and Abigail May. Her father was an early leader and advocate of the Transcendentalist movement, and her mother was an advocate of women's suffrage and abolition. The Alcotts moved to Boston in 1838, where Amos Alcott established the controversial Temple School and joined the Transcendental Club, which counted Ralph Waldo Emerson and Henry David Thoreau as members. Amos Alcott's unique ideas on education and contentious views on child-rearing had a profound effect on his children. These unusual parenting skills and strange ideologies would foster an overriding desire in Louisa May to achieve perfection throughout her life. Her often contemptuous and free-spirited nature would also create conflict within the family. The Alcotts moved to Concord, Massachusetts, in 1840. It was here that she become friends with Ralph Waldo Emerson and Henry David Thoreau, whom she often accompanied on walks in the countryside. During this period, other notable transcendentalists and free thinkers, such as Margaret Fuller and Nathaniel Hawthorne, were frequent guests at the Alcott home.

Orchard House, the home of Louisa May Alcott in Concord, Massachusetts.

By 1845, the Alcott family had purchased "The Orchard House" estate on Lexington Road in Concord. This home, which was surrounded by apple orchards, would later serve as the setting for Alcott's novel, *Little Women* (1868-69) and its sequels. At the age of fifteen, Louisa May began to contribute to the family income by working various jobs; these experiences would later inspire another novel, *Work: A Story of Experience* (1873). While she always kept a journal, Alcott was also encouraged to

NOVELIST

Born: Germantown, Pennsylvania

Died: Boston, Massachusetts

Buried: Sleepy Hollow Cemetery

Concord, Massachusetts

Gravesite of Louisa May Alcott at Sleepy Hollow Cemetery, Concord, Massachusetts.

write poetry and plays. Some of her first poems were published anonymously or under the pseudonym "A.N. Barnard." Most notable among these was *Flower Fables* (1854), which was written for Ellen Emerson, the daughter of Ralph Waldo Emerson.

During the Civil War, Alcott served for a short time as a nurse at the Union Hospital in Washington, D.C. Her letters home were later revised and printed in the New England anti-slavery newspaper, *The Commonwealth*, and were later published as *Hospital Sketches* (1863). This work, which was well-received, detailed the negligence and insensitive conduct of doctors in these military hospitals. In the following years, Alcott became active in reform movements, fighting for the abolition of slavery and for women's rights. At this point, she began to write full-time, publishing such works as *The Rose Family: A Fairy Tale* (1864), *Moods* (1865), and *A Long Fatal Love Chase* (1866). Her publisher, Thomas Niles, requested she write "a girl's story," resulting in *Little Women* (1868). The novel follows the lives of four sisters, Meg, Jo, Beth, and Amy March, and is loosely based on Alcott's childhood experiences with her three sisters. *Little Women* was a novel written for girls that veered from conventional styles. The major themes of the novel, domesticity, work, and true love, are all mutually dependent, and each is necessary in order to achieve the individual identities of the four main characters. *Little Women* was a commercial and critical success, which prompted Alcott to write the sequel, *Good Wives* (1869). These two novels would later be combined into one work. Alcott followed these successes with two more sequels also featuring the March sisters: *Little Men* (1871) and *Jo's Boys* (1886). Other works during this period included *An Old-Fashioned Girl* (1870), *Eight Cousins* (1875) and its sequel, *Rose in Bloom* (1876), *A Modern Mephistopheles* (1877), *Under the Lilacs* (1879), and *Jack and Jill* (1880).

Alcott moved to Boston in the late 1880s and continued to write novels, including *A Garland for Girls* (1888) and other works. She never married, had no children, and suffered from numerous health issues. On March 6, 1888, two days after the death of her father, Louisa May suffered a stroke and died at her Boston home. Her last words were alleged to be: "Is it not meningitis?" She was buried within the family plot atop Author's Ridge at Sleepy Hollow Cemetery in Concord, Massachusetts. Some biographers attributed her health issues and death to mercury poisoning. During service in the Civil War, she contracted typhoid fever and was treated with a compound that contained mercury. Recent analysis of Alcott's illness, however, suggests that her chronic health problems might have been associated with an autoimmune disease, and not acute mercury exposure. Moreover, a late portrait of Alcott shows rashes on her cheeks, which is a symptom of lupus.

"The reports of my death are greatly exaggerated."

MARK TWAIN

Mark Twain
(1835-1910)

Mark Twain was a talented writer and speaker who was a master at crafting amusing stories that were filled with irony and sarcasm. Through informal speech and plain language, he disarmed his readers and presented an authentic depiction of his times. Many of his works were censored or banned. During his lifetime, Twain published dozens of books, hundreds of essays, numerous articles, reviews, and short stories, many of which are still in print today.

Mark Twain's birthplace in Florida, Missouri (undated photograph). *Courtesy of the Library of Congress, Prints & Photographs Division, LC-B2-6046-1.*

Boyhood home of Mark Twain in Hannibal, Missouri.

Mark Twain, circa 1907. *Courtesy of the Library of Congress, Prints & Photographs Division, LC-USZ62-5513.*

NOVELIST, SHORT STORY WRITER & ESSAYIST

Born: Florida, Missouri

Died: Redding, Connecticut

Buried: Woodlawn Cemetery, Elmira, New York

He was born Samuel Langhorne Clemens on November 30, 1835, in Florida, Missouri, the son of John Marshall Clemens and Jane Lampton. His birth would coincide with the closest approach to Earth of Halley's Comet. He spent his early childhood in nearby Hannibal, Missouri, located on the banks of the Mississippi River. There he observed the riverboat town, and was captivated by its romance, but was also disgusted by its brutality. His father died in 1847 and to help the family, eleven-year-old Samuel went to work as a store clerk and a delivery boy. He also found employment at a local printer and occasionally wrote articles for a local newspaper. In 1852, he wrote a humorous article, "The Dandy Frightening the Squatter," that was published by a sportsmen's magazine in Boston, Massachusetts.

Mark Twain's home in Hartford, Connecticut. *Courtesy of the Library of Congress, Prints & Photographs Division, LC-HS503-1866.*

In the coming years, Clemens traveled throughout the Midwest and East Coast working as a journeyman printer. He dreamed of making his fortune in South America beside the fertile banks of the Amazon River. Instead, he traveled down the Mississippi River as a riverboat pilot, a position he held until the outbreak of the Civil War. He headed west in 1861, traveling on a stagecoach across the Great Plains and the Rocky Mountains, stopping in Salt Lake City. These frontier experiences would inspire future works, such as *Roughing It* (1872) and "The Celebrated Jumping Frog of Calaveras County" (1865). His western journey ended in Virginia City, Nevada, where, for a short time, he tried his hand at mining. Failing as a miner, he turned to journalism and wrote articles for a Virginia City newspaper, *The Territorial Enterprise*. On February 3, 1863, Clemens first began using the famous pseudonym Mark Twain. He claimed that the name was derived from his years working on the Mississippi, explaining that mark twain was riverboat language, where two fathoms (a depth indicating safe water for passage of a boat) was measured on the sounding line and "twain" was an old term for two. The river boatman's cry was "by the mark twain," meaning according to the mark on the line, the depth was two fathoms, or the water was twelve feet deep and safe to pass.

By 1864, Twain had moved further west to San Francisco, where he continued to write and, in 1865, published his first successful short story, "The Celebrated Jumping Frog of Calaveras County." This story brought him national acclaim and the following year, the *Sacramento Union* asked him to write a series of articles about a new excursion service to Hawaii. These articles were widely read and provided the basis for a successful series of lectures. The talks were posthumously collected and published as *Letters from the Sandwich Islands* (1938) and *Letters from Honolulu* (1939). Between 1866 and 1867, Twain worked for numerous newspapers, including *The Alta California*. He also traveled to the Mediterranean, where he wrote a collection of travelogues that were later published as *The Innocents Abroad* (1869). It was on this expedition that he met his future brother-in-law, Charles Langdon. Both were passengers aboard the *Quaker City* on their way to the Holy Land. Langdon showed Twain a photograph of his sister, Olivia, with which Twain claimed to have fallen in love at first sight.

Twain was formally introduced to her in December 1867 in New York City. On their first outing together, they attended a reading by Charles Dickens. Olivia turned down his first proposal of marriage, but finally accepted in November 1868. They were married on February 2, 1870, in Elmira, New York. They then moved to Buffalo, New York, where Twain owned a stake in the *Buffalo Express* newspaper and worked as an editor and writer. While living in Buffalo, their young son, Langdon, died of diphtheria (an upper respiratory infection). They also had three daughters: Suzy, Clara, and Jean. In 1871, they moved to Hartford, Connecticut,

Gravesite monument to Mark Twain at Woodlawn Cemetery in Elmira, New York.

where Twain continued to write, publishing *Roughing It* (1872), an account of his travels in Nevada. In 1875, he wrote *The Adventures of Tom Sawyer,* which was a fictionalized account of his boyhood memories of life along the Mississippi River. He also published *The Prince and the Pauper* (1882), *A Connecticut Yankee in King Arthur's Court* (1889), and *The Adventures of Huckleberry Finn* (1885), which is almost universally acknowledged as being one of the best novels in American literature. It is celebrated for its setting and characters, and its satirical depiction of Southern society and racism. It was the first major American novel to be written totally in language characterized by local dialect. Ernest Hemingway once said that "all American literature begins with this book."

During his lifetime, Twain would make a fortune through his literary endeavors, but also lost a great deal through bad investments. Family friend Henry Huttleston Rogers, an executive at Standard Oil, suggested that Twain file for bankruptcy and transfer the copyrights on his books to his wife. Rogers took over Twain's finances until all creditors were repaid. In July of 1895, Twain embarked on a year-long, worldwide lecture tour to pay off his creditors. The tour was long and demanding, and took a personal toll on his health.

In the last decade of his life, Twain's attitude and writings became more and more bitter, particularly after his beloved wife's death in 1904. His works during this period included *The Man That Corrupted Hadleyburg* (1900) and *Eve's Diary* (1906). He then began to dictate his autobiography, excerpts of which were published in magazines in late 1906. With the income from the autobiography, Twain built a home in Redding, Connecticut, which was named "Stormfield." In 1909, tragedies, such as the deaths of his youngest daughter, Jean, and old friend, Henry Rogers, threw him into a deep depression. Twain infamously prophesied his own death by stating: "I came in with Halley's Comet in 1835. It is coming again next year, and I expect to go out with it. It will be the greatest disappointment of my life if I don't go out with Halley's Comet. The Almighty has said, no doubt: 'Now here are these two unaccountable freaks; they came in together, they must go out together.'"

Twain's prophecy was accurate, and on April 21, 1910, the day after Halley's Comet came closest to the Earth, he died from a heart attack at his home in Redding, Connecticut. His funeral was held at the "Old Brick" Presbyterian Church in New York City, and he was buried within his wife's family plot at Woodlawn Cemetery in Elmira, New York. His grave is marked by a twelve-foot monument, placed there by his surviving daughter, Clara.

Close-up view of Mark Twain's grave marker.

Henry James
(1843-1916)

Henry James, circa 1910-1915. *Courtesy of the Library of Congress, Prints and Photographs Division, George G. Bain Collection, LC-B2-3041-15.*

NOVELIST & SHORT STORY WRITER

Born: New York City, New York

Died: London, England

Buried: Cambridge Cemetery, Cambridge, Massachusetts

"Three things in human life are important. The first is to be kind. The second is to be kind. And the third is to be kind."

HENRY JAMES

Henry James was one of the leading advocates of the 19th-century literary school of realism. Many of his early works were serialized in *The Atlantic Monthly*. They included narrative romances with complicated characters and discussed subjects ranging from politics to social status, with themes of personal liberties, feminism, and ethics. A committed bachelor, James would live much of his life in Europe, becoming a British citizen in 1915 after the outbreak of World War I. Many of his works were later adapted for the stage and screen.

He was born Henry James Jr. on April 15, 1843, in New York City, the son of theologian Henry James Sr. and Mary Robertson Walsh. James' father was one of the foremost intellectuals of his time, and was friends with well-known transcendentalists, such as Ralph Waldo Emerson and Henry David Thoreau. Education and travel were very important to Henry James Sr., and the family would spend many years in Europe where his children were tutored in the best schools.

Henry James Jr. would briefly attend Harvard College and study law, but quickly became bored with the subject matter. He published his first short story, "A Tragedy of Error" (1864), at the age of 21 and then devoted himself to full-time writing. In the coming years, he traveled extensively, wrote book reviews, and submitted short stories to magazines, such as the *North American Review*, *The Nation*, *North American Tribune*, *Macmillan's*, and *The Atlantic Monthly*. The latter would serialize his first novel *Watch and Ward* (1871).

In 1876, James left the United States and lived for a brief time in Paris, before moving permanently to England. During these years, he wrote novels about Americans living abroad. Classic novels of this period include *Daisy Miller* (1879), *The Portrait of a Lady* (1881), and *The Bostonians* (1886). In 1897, he left London for a quieter existence in Rye, East Sussex, where he purchased "Lamb House." It was here he would write *What Maisie Knew* (1897), *The Wings of the Dove* (1902), and the novella *The Turn of the Screw* (1898). In 1904, he traveled back to the United States and embarked on a successful lecture tour, which would later inspire a series of essays that would be published in several magazines.

On July 26, 1915, James officially became a British citizen. He felt compelled to declare his loyalty to Britain in protest of America's refusal to enter World War I. Four months later, on December 2, 1915, he suffered a minor stroke, which caused his writing to diminish. On January 1, 1916, he was awarded the Order of Merit by King George V. Over the next few months, his health steadily declined and on February 28, 1916, he died from pneumonia at his home in London. His remains were cremated at Golders Green Crematorium and the ashes were returned to the United States and interred at the Cambridge Cemetery in Cambridge, Massachusetts. James' marker is inscribed: "Novelist, citizen of two countries, interpreter of his generation on both sides of the sea." In 1976, a memorial marker was placed within Poets' Corner at Westminster Abbey.

Lamb House, in Rye, East Sussex, was the home of Henry James from 1898 until his death in 1916.

Gravesite of Henry James at the Cambridge Cemetery in Cambridge, Massachusetts.

Henry James' memorial cenotaph at Poets' Corner in Westminster Abbey.

Stephen Crane
(1871–1900)

Stephen Crane, circa 1896.

NOVELIST, POET, SHORT STORY WRITER & JOURNALIST

Born: Newark, New Jersey

Died: Badenweiler, Germany

Buried: Evergreen Cemetery, Hillside, New Jersey

"You cannot choose your battlefield, God does that for you; but you can plant a standard where a standard never flew."

STEPHEN CRANE

Stephen Crane was one of the most innovative writers of his generation, but only two decades after his death, he was nearly forgotten. He was one of the principal writers of the American schools of Realism, Naturalism, and Impressionism in the late 19th century, and his writing was characterized by vivid descriptions and distinctive dialects. Although he is primarily known for the classic novel *The Red Badge of Courage* (1895), Crane was also a prolific short story writer. His writing made a deep impression on 20th-century writers, such as Ernest Hemingway.

Stephen Townley Crane was born on November 1, 1871, in Newark, New Jersey, the youngest child of Jonathan Townley Crane and Mary Helen Peck. His father was a well-known Methodist minister and his mother was an outspoken supporter of the Women's Christian Temperance Union. As a child, Stephen was afflicted with numerous health issues, but despite his physical frailty, Crane was an intelligent child who taught himself to read before the age of four. On February 16, 1880, Reverend Crane died and Stephen was sent to live with his older brother.

In the fall of 1885, Crane was enrolled at Pennington Seminary, near Trenton, New Jersey, but left two years later for Claverack College. He would later reflect upon his time at Claverack as the happiest of his life. There he excelled at military training; this education would later help with the technical writing of *The Red Badge of Courage* (1895). Despite excelling at military studies, he

Stephen Crane's birthplace in Newark, New Jersey (circa 1936). *Courtesy of the Library of Congress, Prints & Photographs Division, HABS NJ, 7-NEARK, 121.*

54

was persuaded to give up a possible career in the army and pursue a degree in engineering at Lafayette College in Easton, Pennsylvania. After only one semester, he transferred to Syracuse University. In 1891, he declared college "a waste of time" and decided to become a full-time writer and reporter.

In the fall of 1891, he moved to Lake View, New Jersey, but made frequent trips into New York City. He then began writing about the impoverished tenement districts of the city. He focused most of his attention on a southern district of Manhattan, known as the Bowery. After the Civil War, the fancy shops and mansions of the Bowery had given way to saloons and brothels, which Crane frequented. He contributed feature articles to various New York newspapers, but struggled to make a steady income.

In October 1892, he moved into a boarding house in Manhattan and, believing nothing honest had been written about the Bowery, was determined to do so himself. His first novel was *Maggie: A Girl of the Streets* (1893). Because of its controversial themes, it was considered offensive, but today it is generally considered to be the first work of the American literary school of Naturalism. Because no one would publish it, Crane decided to do it himself with money he had inherited from his mother. The novel was published in late spring 1893, but despite early critical acclaim, the book sold poorly. Crane later explained his disappointment: "I looked forward to (its) publication and pictured the sensation I thought it would make. It fell flat. Nobody seemed to notice it or care for it...Poor Maggie! She was one of my first loves."

Crane soon became preoccupied with the American Civil War, but was frustrated with stories about it, which he perceived to be unimaginative and poorly written. He commented, "I wonder that some of those fellows don't tell how they felt in those scraps. They spout enough of what they did, but they're as emotionless as rocks." Eventually, he became obsessed with the idea of writing a realistic war novel, which ultimately became *The Red Badge of Courage*. The novel was told from the point of view of a young private, who is, at first, filled with foolish dreams of glory, but quickly becomes disillusioned by the realities of war. Crane would later admit that the first paragraphs came to him with "every word in place, every comma, every period fixed."

By the spring of 1894, Crane had completed the novel and offered the manuscript to the leading magazine for Civil War literature, *McClure's*. While *McClure's* delayed in giving him an answer, they offered him an opportunity to write about the Pennsylvania coal mines. After discovering that *McClure's* could not afford to pay him, he took his novel to Irving Bacheller, who agreed to serially publish it in the *Philadelphia Press*. In October 1895, *The Red Badge of Courage* was published in book form by D. Appleton & Company. Although some critics considered the work overly graphic and profane, it was widely heralded for its realistic portrayal of war and its unique style. The novel has been anthologized numerous times, including in Ernest Hemingway's 1942 collection *Men at War: The Best War Stories of All Time*. In the introduction, Hemingway wrote that the novel "is one of the finest books of our literature."

Wanting to capitalize on the success of the novel, *McClure's* offered Crane a contract to write a series on Civil War battlefields. Crane visited many sites in Northern Virginia. At the end of January 1895, he began a tour of the western United States, and wrote feature articles for Irving Bacheller's syndicate of newspapers. He returned to New York five months later and wrote two more novels: *The Third Violet* and *George's Mother*.

Reveling in his recent success, Crane soon became involved in a highly publicized scandal involving an alleged prostitute named Dora Clark. On the evening of September 16, 1896, Crane was observed escorting Clark and two other women from New York's Broadway Garden. He would later state that he had interviewed the women for an upcoming article. As Crane saw one woman safely to a streetcar, a policeman named Charles Becker arrested the other two women on suspicion of sexual solicitation. Crane attempted to intervene, but was threatened with arrest. Against legal advice, he made a statement confirming Dora Clark's innocence, stating that, "I only know that while with me she acted respectably, and that the policeman's charge was false." On the basis of Crane's testimony, Clark was discharged. The Stephen Crane story, as it became known, quickly became a source for mockery. A couple of weeks after the incident, Dora Clark pressed charges of false arrest. The next day, she was physically assaulted by Charles Becker in the presence of witnesses. Crane, who initially went to Philadelphia to escape the scandal, returned to New York to give his testimony. In retaliation, the police raided his apartment and interviewed friends and acquaintances, in an attempt to find incriminating evidence and damage his reputation. Becker's defense attorneys sought to portray Crane as a man of dubious morals, while the prosecution proved that he frequented brothels. Crane acknowledged that he did visit these establishments, but claimed that it was only for research purposes. Officer Becker was eventually acquitted of the charges, and Crane's reputation was in ruins.

With very few options, Crane was approached by Irving Bacheller to write about the approaching Cuban conflict. He left New York on November 27, 1896, bound for Jacksonville, Florida. Upon arrival, he registered at the St. James Hotel under the alias of Samuel Carleton to maintain anonymity while seeking passage to Cuba. Within days, he met 31-year-old Cora Taylor, owner of the Hotel de Dream. Born into a respectable Boston family, Taylor had been in Jacksonville for several years living a carefree lifestyle, but was also a well-known and respected local figure. She and Crane would spend a lot of time together while he awaited his departure. He was finally cleared to leave for Cuba on New Year's Eve 1896, aboard the S.S. *Commodore*.

The ship sailed with a cargo of supplies and ammunition for the Cuban rebels. Less than two miles from port, the ship struck a sandbar and damaged its hull. Although towed off the sandbar the following day, it was again beached and damaged further. A leak in the boiler room resulted in a breakdown of the water pumps, and the ship began to take on water about sixteen miles from Mosquito Inlet. The lifeboats were lowered in the early morning of January 2, 1897, and the ship ultimately sank. Crane was one of the last to leave the ship and he would later describe the event in the short story "The Open Boat." Crane and three other men floated off the coast of Florida for a day and a half before attempting to land near Daytona Beach. The tiny boat overturned in the rough surf, forcing the men to swim to shore; one of them drowned. The disaster was widely reported in newspapers across the country, and rumors that the ship had been sabotaged were spread, but never substantiated. Portrayed favorably by the press, Crane emerged from the ordeal with his reputation improved, if not completely restored.

Despite the need for rest following this ordeal, Crane soon left Jacksonville and returned to New York City, where he wrote "The Open Boat." By this time, blockades had formed along the Florida coast and Crane concluded that he would never be able to travel to Cuba as a freelance writer. Determined to work as a war correspondent, Crane signed on with William Randolph Hearst's *New York Journal* to cover the looming Greco-Turkish War. He brought along Cora Taylor, who had recently sold her hotel in Florida. They arrived in Greece in early April, and he began to write about the war. An armistice was signed between Greece and Turkey on May 20th, ending the month-long war, and Crane traveled to England.

Crane and Taylor settled in Oxted, England, and began referring to themselves as Mr. and Mrs. Crane. He, however, chose to conceal the relationship from his friends and family in the United States. Negative reviews of his recently published *The Third Violet* (1897) were causing his literary reputation to decline. Reviewers were also critical of his war letters, deeming them self-centered. Although *The Red Badge of Courage* had, by this time, gone through numerous printings, Crane was running out of money. To survive financially, he worked at a feverish pace, writing for any newspaper or magazine that would publish his articles.

At the onset of the Spanish American War in the spring of 1898, Crane was offered a job as a correspondent for *Blackwood's Magazine*. At this same time, his health was deteriorating, and symptoms of tuberculosis, which he had contracted in childhood, were worsening. With almost no income, Crane accepted the assignment and left England for New York, while Taylor remained in England fending off creditors. He arrived in Key West, Florida, two days before Congress declared war with Spain. In June 1898, he was present when U.S. Marines seized Guantanamo Bay. He wrote candidly about his fear during the battle. After showing a willingness to help out during fighting at Cuzco, Cuba, Crane was officially honored for heroism for carrying messages between the lines of battle. In early July, he came down with malaria and yellow fever and was sent back to the United States for medical treatment. Although he had written more than twenty articles in the three months he had covered the war, *Blackwood's* believed that they had not gotten enough material and fired him. After recovering from his health issues, Crane signed with William Randolph Hearst's *New York Journal* and asked to return to Cuba. He intermittently sent out dispatches and stories, but the limited money he got from these articles was not enough to sustain him. He soon left Cuba and traveled back to England.

Upon returning to England, Crane and Taylor relocated to Sussex, but their money problems continued. Deciding that he could no longer afford to write for American publications, he concentrated on publishing in English magazines. He wrote at a feverish pace during these first months, but his health continued to worsen. On December 29, 1899, he suffered a hemorrhage of the lungs, but recovered sufficiently enough to work on a new novel, *The O'Ruddy*. Although plans were made for him to travel as a correspondent to Gibraltar at the

Stephen Crane lived in this home in Brede Place, near Rye, Sussex, England, in the last years of his brief life.

end of March, he suffered two more massive hemorrhages. In late May 1900, Crane traveled to a sanatorium in the Black Forest of Badenweiler, Germany, where he died on June 5, 1900. In his will he left everything to Taylor, who had his remains returned to the United States for burial at Evergreen Cemetery in Hillside, New Jersey.

After Crane's death, Cora returned to Jacksonville, Florida, where she built a successful brothel. On June 1, 1905, she married Hammond P. McNeill, the 25-year-old son of a prominent South Carolina family. He was also the nephew of Anna McNeill Whistler, who was the model for the famous painting known as *Whistler's Mother*. McNeill was later charged with killing one of his wife's lovers, and, following his acquittal, the couple divorced. In the coming years, Cora became a regular contributor to magazines, such as *Harpers Weekly*. She died from a stroke on September 5, 1910, and was buried at Evergreen Cemetery in Jacksonville, Florida.

Grave of Stephen Crane at Evergreen Cemetery in Hillside, New Jersey.

Part Two

The Celebrated Authors of American Literature

in the 20ᵗʰ Century

American literature of the 20th century can be defined by the traditions it defied rather than any it created. Set into motion by rapid changes to the foundations of American lifestyles, literature of this period mirrored these changes, but never fully answered many of the universal questions that were posed. It was during this same period of sweeping changes that American literature finally came into its own within the academic community. The works of American authors, such as Mark Twain and Herman Melville, as well as many others, were at last being taught as subjects of scholarly study at universities, and this helped bolster America's literary standing throughout the world.

Many American writers of the early 20th century abandoned long-established social norms and customs that had been in effect since the Revolutionary period. Advances in technology and social theory, as well as two global wars, helped change the world forever. The growth of industry and a move from an agrarian to an urban culture further eroded the country's founding tenets. America became a nation of factories, with citizens who lived by the products they made rather than the food they grew. These rapid changes helped sow seeds of distrust within America's intellectual and literary communities and helped promote the development of new literary styles. These literary changes of the new century were summed up by poet Ezra Pound, who stated: "Make it New."

Perhaps drawn to poetry's spontaneous nature and its emotionally charged language, many of America's early 20th century writers were poets. These men and women would give modern American poetry a distinctive voice, much like Walt Whitman and others had done in the previous century. From the complex poetic writings of Robert Frost to the avant-garde stylistic innovations of such writers as E.E. Cummings and T.S. Eliot, these Modernist poets tried to describe their profound dissatisfaction with the traditions of past generations.

The American novelists and short story writers of the early 20th century also felt a need to create new forms of literary communication. Ernest Hemingway's novels and short stories often dealt with the realities of war, while his simple, journalistic style of writing expressed a depressing view of the world, where simple cause-and-effect relationships often lacked both reason and philosophy. Similarly, the novels of William Faulkner had multiple points of view, contained complex sentence structure, and stream-of-consciousness narration. The works of these and other writers of this generation often expressed a view of a world that was capable of both amazing technology and unfathomable cruelty.

The literary revolution of the period was not limited to the ideas and styles of poets and novelists. Other writers challenged gender discrimination: Gertrude Stein and Willa Cather shattered the stereotypical images of women with their presence on the literary scene, while other authors wrote about the complications of America's new financial landscape following World War I and the Great Depression. John Steinbeck's novels, such as *Cannery Row* and *Of Mice and Men*, examined the hardships of tenant farmers in California, while F. Scott Fitzgerald's *The Great Gatsby* discussed the widening income gap between the upper classes of society and everyone else.

Before and after World War II, a new generation of extraordinary novelists, poets, and playwrights began to emerge. Their ethnicity, regionalism, and societal characterizations were very different from those of the preceding generation of writers. Chief among them was Robert Penn Warren, who published influential fiction and poetry. His *All the King's Men* was one of the best American political novels of the era and won the 1947 Pulitzer Prize. Many of these writers had been deeply affected by the horrors of the war and the threat of total destruction following the use of the atomic bomb. These writers found the common styles of realism insufficient in describing the nightmarish consequences of the war. Among these novelists were Kurt Vonnegut Jr., whose *Slaughterhouse-*

Five (1969) described the Allied firebombing of the German city of Dresden with a mixture of dark fantasy and unfeeling humor. Though the social climate of the postwar literary period was basically conservative in nature, some of the non-conformist writers of the period included Jack Kerouac, J.D Salinger, and John Updike. Their writings emphasized the development of the sullen, brooding outsider character.

In the South, post-World War II writers would inherit the rich literary legacy of William Faulkner. Many of these were women; especially noteworthy was Flannery O'Connor, who created a blend of comedy and ethical absurdity in her short stories. Other fine writers in the Southern tradition included Truman Capote, who published *In Cold Blood* (1966), a harsh but impressive piece of documentary realism that used many of the techniques of fiction.

The development of cynicism towards the ideals of earlier generations was rapid in its growth and wide-ranging in scope for this generation of writers. They now looked inward to answer questions about religion, sexuality, and other issues. In danger of dissolving itself into generality with its vast blending of literary styles and dealing with a variety of topics, this introspective view was the true hallmark of American literature during the early 20th century. By attempting to rethink their relationship to society and social institutions, these authors and poets shifted the focus of their writing from merely recording what they witnessed in the world to social commentary on the world in general.

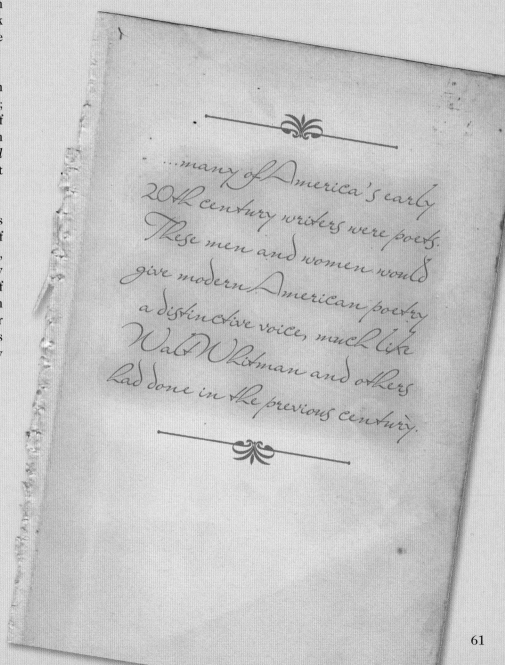

...many of America's early 20th century writers were poets. These men and women would give modern American poetry a distinctive voice, much like Walt Whitman and others had done in the previous century.

L. Frank Baum
(1856–1919)

L. Frank Baum, circa 1908. *Courtesy of the Library of Congress, Prints & Photographs Division, LC-USZ62-103206.*

CHILDREN'S NOVELIST

Born: Chittenango, New York

Died: Hollywood, California

Buried: Forest Lawn Memorial Park
Glendale, California

"Imagination has brought mankind through the dark ages to its present state of civilization. Imagination led Columbus to discover America. Imagination led Franklin to discover electricity."

L. FRANK BAUM

Best known for his series of books about the imaginary Land of Oz, Lyman Frank Baum was born on May 15, 1856, in Chittenango, New York, the child of Benjamin Ward Baum and Cynthia Ann Stanton. Frank, as he preferred to be called, often spent time reading in his father's library, rather than socializing with neighborhood children.

He developed a dislike for the usual scary creatures and violence of traditional children's stories of the period, and would end up creating his own adaptations of these tales in order to give children joy, rather than gloomy and frightening moral lessons.

The birthplace of author L. Frank Baum in Chittenango, New York.

In 1869, at the age of 12, Baum was sent to the Peekskill Military Academy. The atmosphere at Peekskill was intense, and because the strenuous activity was too much for him physically, he was allowed to go home. The experience left him with a dislike for the military and school in general, but he continued to develop a great love of writing. To foster his son's creativity, Benjamin Baum bought a printing press. Together with his younger siblings, Frank started *The Rose Lawn Home Journal* (named after the family estate). He named himself chief writer and editor and his articles, editorials, fiction, and poetry filled its pages.

At the age of 25, Baum moved to New York City to study theater, and from 1881 to 1882, he managed an opera house (built by his father) in Richburg, New York. On November 9, 1882, he married Maud Gage, the daughter of Matilda Joslyn Gage, a leading suffragette. Together they would have four children. In July 1888, giving up on a theater career, Baum moved to Aberdeen, South Dakota, where he opened a general store he called Baum's Bazaar. An unsuccessful business owner, he eventually filed for bankruptcy. Because finances were tight, Baum sought employment as a writer and editor at a local newspaper, *The Aberdeen Saturday Pioneer*. In 1891, he moved to Chicago, and more business failures followed. Encouraged by his mother-in-law, Baum began to write down the nursery rhymes he had told to his children over the years. In 1897, these stories became *Mother Goose in Prose*. The book was well-received and, two years later, he collaborated with cartoonist William Wallace Denslow on yet another successful children's book, *Father Goose: His Book* (1899).

In 1900, he wrote and published what would become one of the most beloved children's books of all-time, *The Wonderful Wizard of Oz*. The novel follows the adventures of a young girl named Dorothy Gale, who, after being swept away from her Kansas farm by a tornado, finds herself in the magical Land of Oz. The novel was a critical and financial success, and was one of the best-selling children's books for many years after its initial publication. Baum's intention with the Wizard of Oz books was to make the characters non-stereotypical. Although these early books contained some violence, his later works were less cruel in nature. His books are often cited as the beginning of the refinement of children's stories, although he did not do a great deal more than eliminate harsh moral lessons. Baum also intentionally left out any reference to romantic love in his stories, which he considered to be uninteresting and largely beyond the comprehension of young children. The next book in the series was *The Land of Oz*, (1904), followed by *Ozma of Oz*, (1907), *Dorothy and the Wizard in Oz* (1908), and *The Road to Oz* (1909). In all, Baum would write thirteen novels based on the places and people of the Land of Oz.

In 1910, Baum moved to Hollywood, California, and continued to write, penning several children's stories that included *The Sea Fairies* (1911) and *Sky Island* (1912). He began referring to himself as the "Royal Historian of Oz" and wrote one Oz book per year. He also started the Oz Film Manufacturing Company. On May 5, 1919, after several years of declining health, Baum suffered a stroke at his home in Hollywood, California. He died the next day and his alleged last words were, "now we can cross the shifting sands." Baum was buried at Forest Lawn Memorial Park in Glendale, California. In 1920, his final Oz book, *Glinda of Oz*, was published posthumously. After her husband's death, Maud Baum authorized Ruth Plumly Thompson to write more Oz sequels. She also helped promote MGM's 1939 film *The Wizard of Oz*. On March 6, 1953, Maud Gage Baum died at age 91, having survived him by 34 years. She was buried beside her husband at Forest Lawn Memorial Park.

Gravesite of L. Frank Baum at Forest Lawn Memorial Park, Glendale, California.

O. Henry
(1862–1910)

William Sydney Porter, "O. Henry," circa 1890.

SHORT STORY WRITER

Born: Greensboro, North Carolina

Died: New York City, New York

Buried: Riverside Cemetery, Asheville, North Carolina

"Write what you like; there is no other rule."

O. HENRY

Prolific short story author William Sydney Porter was born on September 11, 1862, in Greensboro, North Carolina, the son of Algernon Sidney Porter, a physician, and Mary Jane Swain. His mother died from tuberculosis when he was a small child, and he was raised by his paternal grandmother and aunt. In 1876, he graduated from his Aunt Evelina Maria Porter's elementary school and then went to work as an apprentice at his uncle's drugstore. In 1881, at the age of 19, he became a licensed pharmacist and, in his spare time, drew sketches of the store's patrons.

Home of William Sydney Porter in Austin, Texas.

In 1882, Porter moved to Texas to help alleviate a persistent cough and other health issues. By 1884, his health had improved and Porter traveled to Austin, Texas, where he found work as a pharmacist, draftsman, bank teller, and journalist. He also began to write short stories. During this period, he met his future wife, Athol Estes. Because of her ongoing health issues associated with tuberculosis, her parents strongly objected to their daughter's new relationship. On July 1, 1887, Porter and Estes eloped. Throughout their marriage, Athol was an enthusiastic supporter of her husband's writing, and together they would have two children.

Porter began working at the First National Bank of Austin in 1891. The bank was operated informally and Porter, who was employed as the bookkeeper, was apparently careless in keeping records. In 1894, he was accused of embezzling funds from the bank and was relieved of his duties, but no other action was taken. During this same period, he contributed short stories and sketches to *The Rolling Stone*, a national magazine that featured stories about real life and politics. Porter's writing soon caught the attention of the editor of *The Houston Post* and he was offered a position as a columnist at the newspaper. Porter found ideas for his articles by observing the activities of everyday people, a technique he would use throughout his entire writing career.

Unknown to Porter at the time, his former employer, the First National Bank of Austin, was being audited by federal bank inspectors. They soon uncovered the fund shortages that had led to his firing, and a federal indictment of embezzlement was filed against Porter. On July 7, 1896, a day before he was to stand trial, Porter skipped town and fled, first to New Orleans, and later to Honduras. While on the run in Central America, he wrote several short story collections that included *Cabbages and Kings*, in which he coined the phrase "banana republic," which became a popular synonym for unstable Latin American countries. In February 1897, after learning that his wife was dying, Porter voluntarily returned to the United States and surrendered to authorities. Athol Estes Porter died on July 25, 1897, from tuberculosis.

In February 1898, Porter was found guilty of embezzlement and sentenced to five years in prison. On March 25, 1898, he began serving his sentence at the federal prison in Columbus, Ohio. While incarcerated, he continued to write, penning fourteen short stories, which were published under various pseudonyms. A friend in New Orleans forwarded the stories to publishers who had no idea the writer was in prison. The most famous of these pen names, "O. Henry," first appeared on the story "Whistling Dick's Christmas Stocking" in the December 1899 issue of *McClure's Magazine*. On July 24, 1901, Porter was paroled after serving three years of a five-year sentence. Upon his release, he officially changed his name to O. Henry. Over the years, he gave various explanations for the origin of his famous pen name. In 1909, he gave an interview to *The New York Times* in which he stated:

It was during these New Orleans days that I adopted my pen name of O. Henry. I said to a friend: "I'm going to send out some stuff. I don't know if it amounts to much, so I want to get a literary alias. Help me pick out a good one." He suggested that we get a newspaper and pick a name from the first list of notables that we found in it. In the society columns we found the account of a fashionable ball. "Here we have our notables," said he. We looked down the list and my eye lighted on the name Henry. "That'll do for a last name," said I. "Now for a first name, I want something short; none of your three-syllable names for me." "Why don't you use a plain initial letter, then?" asked my friend. "Well," said I, "O is about the easiest letter written, and O it is."

Gravesite of William Sydney Porter at the Riverside Cemetery, Asheville, North Carolina.

He moved to New York City in 1902 and wrote for *The New York World Sunday Magazine*. His collection of short stories, *Cabbages and Kings*, was published two years later. This was followed by *The Four Million* (1906), which included stories, such as "The Gift of the Magi" and "The Furnished Room." In 1910, he published *Whirligigs* (1910), which included one of his best known short stories, "The Ransom of Red Chief." Over his lifetime, he would publish ten collections of short stories, adored by his readers, but often dismissed by critics. His last years were overshadowed by declining health, financial problems, and alcoholism. In 1907, he was briefly married to Sarah Lindsay Coleman, but they separated after a year of marriage. His health continued to deteriorate in the coming years, and on June 5, 1910, he died from cirrhosis of the liver, complications from diabetes, and other ailments. After funeral services in New York City, Henry was buried at the Riverside Cemetery in Asheville, North Carolina. After his death, three collections of his short stories were published: *Sixes and Sevens* (1911), *Rolling Stones* (1912), and *Waifs and Strays* (1917).

Edith Wharton
(1862–1937)

Edith Wharton (circa 1890) by E.F. Cooper at Newport, Rhode Island.
Courtesy of Yale University, Beinecke Rare Book & Manuscript Library.

NOVELIST, SHORT STORY WRITER & POET

Born: New York City, New York

Died: Saint-Brice-sous-Forêt, France

Buried: American Cemetery, Versailles, France

"I have never known a novel that was good enough to be good in spite of its being adapted to the author's political views."

— EDITH WHARTON

Edith Wharton was the first female recipient of the Pulitzer Prize, and many of her novels have been adapted to both stage and screen. However, her notorious first encounter with author F. Scott Fitzgerald, whom she pronounced as "awful" in her diary, has become a literary legend. She was born Edith Newbold Jones on January 24, 1862, in New York City, the daughter of George Frederic Jones and Lucretia Rhinelander. When Edith was a small child, her family moved to Europe and spent several years traveling throughout the continent, but by the mid-1870s, her family was back in New York City, where Edith continued her education under private tutors. It was during this period that she began to write short stories and poetry.

In the late 1870s, the Jones family again traveled to Europe, but three years later, George Jones died and the family returned to New York. On April 29, 1885, Edith married Edward Robbins Wharton, who was from a wealthy Philadelphia family. During the first few years of their marriage, the couple traveled extensively, but Edward began to suffer from bouts of severe depression, and their travel was soon curtailed. In 1891, Edith published her first short story in *Scribner's Magazine*.

During her lifetime, Wharton was well-known for her sense of style, penning several books on interior design and gardens, including *The Decoration of Houses* (1897, co-authored by Ogden Codman) and *Italian Villas and their Gardens* (1904). She also wrote numerous short story compilations, which included *The Greater Inclination* (1899), *Crucial Instances* (1901), *The Descent of Man and Other Stories* (1904), *The Hermit and the Wild Woman* (1908), *Xingu and Other Stories* (1917), and *The World Over* (1936). She also penned several ghost stories: *Tales of Men and Ghosts* (1910), *Here and Beyond* (1926), and *Ghosts* (1937).

"The Mount" in Lenox, Massachusetts, was the home of Edith Wharton from 1902-1911.

In 1901, she began the design and construction of a new home called "The Mount" in Lenox, Massachusetts. Edith's niece, Beatrix Ferrand, a landscape architect, helped design the extensive gardens and terraces on the property. During this period, Wharton continued to write and published such works as *The Valley of Decision* (1902), *Sanctuary* (1903), *House of Mirth* (1905), *Madame de Treymes* (1907), and *The Fruit of the Tree* (1907). She then moved to France, which prompted her to write the travel essay "A Motor-Flight through France" (1908). While in Paris, she began an affair with journalist Morton Fullerton, whom she considered an intellectual equal. In 1909, she published a collection of poetry, *Artemis to Actaeon and Other Verses*, followed by several novels that included *Ethan Frome* (1911), *The Reef* (1912), and *The Custom of the Country* (1913). The conflict between societal mores and the pursuit of happiness was a common theme throughout many of Wharton's novels. By 1913, Edward's mental state had deteriorated to the extent that Edith sought a divorce and permanently moved to Paris.

During World War I, Edith helped refugees and orphans in both France and Belgium by raising funds and establishing schools. She also toured battlefields and hospitals, where she often helped with the sick and injured. These experiences were collected in *Fighting France* (1915) and *The Marne* (1918). For her charitable efforts, she was awarded the title of Chevalier (Knight) in the French Legion of Honor in 1916. She continued to write, and published such works as *The Bunner Sisters* (1917) and *Summer* (1917). In 1918, she moved to "Pavillon Colombe" on the outskirts of Paris. There she wrote *French Ways and Their Meaning* (1919) and *The Age of Innocence* (1920), for which she was awarded the Pulitzer Prize. Over the next decade, she wrote numerous novels, including *The Glimpses of the Moon* (1922), *Twilight Sleep* (1927), *Hudson River Bracketed* (1929), *Human Nature* (1933), *A Backward Glance* (1934), and many others. On August 11, 1937, she suffered a stroke and died at Pavillon Colombe. Her funeral service was held at the American Cathedral of the Holy Trinity in Paris, and she was buried at the American Cemetery near Versailles. The epitaph on the cross adorning her grave marker reads "O Crux Ave Spes Unica," which means, "Hail O Cross Our Only Hope."

Theodore Dreiser
(1871–1945)

Theodore Dreiser, circa 1933. *Courtesy of the Library of Congress, Prints & Photographs Division, Carl Van Vechten Collection, LC-USZ62-42486.*

NOVELIST & JOURNALIST

Born: Terre Haute, Indiana
Died: Hollywood, California
Buried: Forest Lawn Memorial Park, Glendale, California

"In order to have wisdom, we must have ignorance."

THEODORE DREISER

Theodore Dreiser used realism to suggest that social conditions, heredity, and environment had profound influence in shaping human nature. His novels often featured characters that achieved their objectives in spite of a lack of morality. He battled against censorship for portrayals of sexual promiscuity. Satirist Henry L. Mencken, a staunch supporter of Dreiser during his lifetime, argued: "No other American of his generation left so wide and handsome a mark upon the national letters. American writing, before and after his time, differed almost as much as biology before and after Darwin. He was a man of large originality, of profound feeling, and of unshakable courage. All of us who write are better off because he lived, worked, and hoped."

Theodore Herman Albert Dreiser was born on August 27, 1871, in Terre Haute, Indiana, the child of John Paul Dreiser and Sarah Maria Schanab. His father had an unstable work history, and because of this, the family suffered from financial hardships. As a child, Theodore stuttered, was very shy, and was bullied by other boys. He hated his father for his harsh discipline and strict Catholic principles, but loved his mother for her whimsical, romantic ideals.

In his early teens, he traveled with his mother to Chicago, where he witnessed firsthand the contrast between small town life and the big city. After a short stay in Illinois, they moved to Warsaw, Indiana, where Theodore's mother had inherited land from her father. In the fall of 1889, Dreiser began attending classes at the University of Indiana, but quickly felt isolated. Uninspired, he withdrew after one year of study and returned home. That fall, his mother died, after which Theodore drifted aimlessly from job to job, searching for some sort of purpose.

In 1892, Dreiser returned to Chicago and began to write. He quickly discovered that his writing was just as good as that of those being published in the newspapers and, in June 1892, he landed a job as an investigative journalist at *The Chicago Globe*. The following year, he traveled to St. Louis to work for *The Globe-Democrat* and *The Republic*, where he gained notoriety for his unique reporting style. In 1893, he was assigned to escort twenty female teachers to Chicago's Columbian Exposition and report on their activities. One of these young ladies, Sara Osborne White, would become his future wife. Dreiser was immediately attracted to the vivacious redhead and soon fell hopelessly in love.

Aching for a chance to fulfill his pressing sexual needs, Dreiser quickly proposed marriage—although limited finances put a quick halt to the wedding plans.

Driven by an overriding desire for fame and fortune, and believing that he could have better success as a writer on his own, Dreiser purchased a small town newspaper in Grand Rapids, Ohio. With promises to send for Sara soon, he boarded a train for Ohio. He arrived to find that the paper was in shambles and there wasn't enough potential to make any money, so he moved on to Toledo, where he sought employment at *The Toledo Blade*. Unfortunately, no permanent opening materialized, and he traveled to Cleveland and Pittsburgh, where he began to write about the labor disputes arising from the Great Homestead Strike of 1892. Moving to New York City, he found employment at Joseph Pulitzer's *The World*, where he wrote about a streetcar strike in Brooklyn. These impressions would later be incorporated into his first novel, *Sister Carrie*. On December 28, 1898, Dreiser married Sara White. The marriage was troubled from the beginning, as he was never able to fully commit himself to just one woman. The two separated in 1909, partly as a result of Dreiser's infatuation with Thelma Cudlipp, the teenage daughter of a colleague, but they never officially divorced because of his devout Catholic beliefs.

While working at *The New York World*, Frank Norris, editor at Doubleday Publishing, helped Dreiser publish his first novel, *Sister Carrie* (1900). When Frank Doubleday read the final draft, he pronounced the book to be immoral and badly written. He wanted to back out of its publication, but Dreiser held firm and *Sister Carrie* was reluctantly printed with a limited press run. He would spend his remaining literary career struggling with editors, publishers, and various political agencies, all of whom tried to make his novels suitable for public consumption. In 1901, Dreiser began writing his second novel, *Jennie Gerhardt*, but frustration with the editing process delayed its publication for nearly ten years. In the coming years, he wrote numerous novels, including *The Financier* (1912) *The Titan* (1914), and *The Genius* (1915). He continued to write for newspapers like *The Saturday Evening Post* and the socialist magazine *The New York Call*.

Dreiser had always viewed criminal activity as a by-product of America's obsession with financial success, and was inspired to write what has been considered his greatest novel, *An American Tragedy* (1925). The novel was loosely based on the 1906 murder of Grace Brown and the later conviction and execution of her lover, Chester Gillette. The murder trial drew international attention and Dreiser studied the case closely. He based his main character, Clyde Griffiths, on Chester Gillette, deliberately giving him the same initials. Although the novel was a critical and commercial success, it was banned in Boston and the legal battles over its publication dragged on for years.

Following the success of *An American Tragedy*, Dreiser was highly sought after by political organizations. In 1927, he made a controversial visit to the Soviet Union. The Soviet government thought that Dreiser's positive view of communism would carry a lot of weight in America. During the visit, he met with various Soviet leaders and wrote extensively. He would continue to promote political activism for the remainder of his life. During the Great Depression, he wrote: "I feel that the immense gulf between wealth and poverty in America and throughout the world should be narrowed. I feel the government should effect the welfare of all the people, not that of a given class."

He wrote very little fiction during the 1930s, devoting most of his time to political activities. During the Spanish Civil War, he became an active supporter of the Popular Front government. In 1939, Dreiser traveled to Washington, D.C. and New York City to lecture on behalf of the Committee for Soviet Friendship and American Peace Mobilization. He was highly critical of the capitalist system and stated: "In my personal judgment, America as yet certainly is neither a social nor a democratic success. Its original democratic theory does not work."

In 1941, he wrote the essay "America is Worth Saving," in which he tried to convince the American public that involvement in the approaching war in Europe should be avoided. After the bombing of Pearl Harbor and America's entrance into the conflict, Dreiser joined the American Communist Party in protest. He summed up his reasons by stating, "Belief in the greatness and dignity of Man has been the guiding principle of my life and work. The logic of my life and work leads me therefore to apply for membership in the Communist Party."

On December 28, 1945, Theodore Dreiser died from a heart attack at his home in West Hollywood, California. He was buried at Forest Lawn Memorial Park in Glendale, California. His last novels, *The Bulwark* (1946) and *The Stoic* (1947), were published after his death.

Grave of Theodore Dreiser and his long-time mistress, Helen Richardson, at Forest Lawn Memorial Park in Glendale, California.

Close-up view of Theodore Dreiser's grave marker.

> *"The fact that I was a girl never damaged my ambitions to be a pope or an emperor."*
>
> WILLA CATHER

Willa Sibert Cather was born on December 7, 1873, in Back Creek Valley, near Winchester, Virginia, the daughter of Charles Fectigue Cather and Mary Virginia Boak. Her childhood was filled with happy memories that would later serve as a foundation for future stories and characters. In 1883, her family moved to Nebraska, where her father worked on a farm. Willa's experience on the frontier would have a profound impact upon her life and her future literary career. She was deeply affected by her natural surroundings, as well as the varied cultures of European-American immigrants and Native Americans. In 1890, she started attending the University of Nebraska, where she initially studied science with the hope of becoming a doctor. During her first year, she wrote an essay that was published in the *Nebraska State Journal.* She became a regular contributor to the magazine, and changed her major to English. She graduated in 1894.

Childhood home of Willa Cather in Red Cloud, Nebraska.

Two years later, she accepted a position as a journalist for the *Home Monthly* magazine in Pittsburgh, Pennsylvania. In 1897, she became an editor and drama critic for the *Pittsburgh Leader* and frequently contributed poetry and short fiction to *The Library,* another local publication. She also taught at Central High School and Allegheny High School, where she became the head of the English department. In 1906, Cather moved to New York City to work in the editorial department of *McClure's Magazine,* where she wrote numerous articles, including a very critical serialized biography of Christian Science founder Mary Baker Eddy. The book was published in 1909 as *The Life of Mary Baker Eddy and the History of Christian Science* (1909). In 1912, she published the novel *Alexander's Bridge,* which was followed by *O Pioneers!* (1913), *The Song of the Lark* (1915), and *My Antonia* (1918). These deeply moving and sentimental works were critical and financial successes.

Willa Cather
(1873–1947)

Willa Cather, circa 1936. *Courtesy of the Library of Congress, Prints & Photographs Division, Carl Van Vechten Collection, LC-USZ62-116087.*

NOVELIST

Born: Back Creek Valley, Virginia
Died: New York City, New York
Buried: The Old Burying Ground
Jaffrey, New Hampshire

Grave of Willa Cather at the Old Burying Ground in Jaffrey, New Hampshire.

In 1922, she was awarded a Pulitzer Prize for her novel *One of Ours*. It is the story of a young man born after the American frontier has vanished, who seeks answers and redemption on the battlefields of France during World War I. In the coming years, Cather would write other novels, including *A Lady Lost* (1923), *The Professor's House* (1925), *My Mortal Enemy* (1926), and *Death Comes for the Archbishop* (1927). By the early 1930s, critics had begun to dismiss her writing as overly romantic and nostalgic. During the Great Depression, her works, such as *Shadow on the Rocks* (1931) and *Lucy Gayheart* (1935), were seen as lacking social relevance. Discouraged by the harsh criticism, she retreated from public life.

Throughout Cather's adult life, her most significant friendships were primarily with women and, today, her sexual identity remains a hot topic among scholars. The most notable of her relationships was with Edith Lewis, and began in the early 1900s. The two women lived together in a series of apartments in New York City for nearly four decades. In the last years of her life, Cather wrote less frequently, but still published works, such as *Sapphira and the Slave Girl* (1940), *The Old Beauty and Others* (1948), a collection of short stories, and *Willa Cather on Writing* (1948), a collection of essays about writing. On April 24, 1947, Cather died from a cerebral hemorrhage at her apartment on Madison Avenue in New York City and was interred at the Old Burying Ground in Jaffrey, New Hampshire. Always a very private person, Cather destroyed most of her personal papers and letters prior to her death. Her will specifically restricted the ability of scholars to quote from any personal papers that remained. In 1956, her estate posthumously released a collection of previously unpublished short stories entitled *Five Stories*. Despite her wishes, *The Selected Letters of Willa Cather* was published in April 2013.

"A writer should write with his eyes and painter paint with his ears."

GERTRUDE STEIN

Gertrude Stein was a very influential literary figure of the early 20th century and greatly affected the writing of a generation of American writers, although the significance of her own literary works has been called into question. She was born on February 3, 1874, in Allegheny, Pennsylvania, the youngest daughter of Daniel and Amelia Stein. As a young child, her family traveled often and they lived for brief periods in Austria and France, eventually settling in San Francisco. Gertrude's early education was very irregular, but she was an avid reader and developed a strong interest in art. In 1888, her mother died, and her father passed away three years later. These tragedies affected Gertrude enormously and led to the splintering of the family, with Gertrude and a younger sister being sent to live with relatives in Baltimore.

In 1893, after finishing only a year of high school, Stein was admitted to Radcliffe College in Massachusetts, where she majored in psychology. She became a favorite of psychologist and philosopher William James, who recognized her intellectual potential. It was James who encouraged Stein to enroll in medical school, although Stein professed she had no interest in the subject. She would spend two years at Johns Hopkins Medical School before withdrawing. In her later writings, she would describe this period as being one of her darkest. She suffered from numerous bouts of depression and struggled with issues of physical appearance, sexuality, and personal identity.

In 1902, Stein relocated to Paris, where she lived with her brother, Leo, and pursued a career in art. Five years later, she met Alice B. Toklas, a fellow American, who became her lifelong companion, lover, and personal secretary. Stein quickly established herself as a staunch supporter of avant-garde painters, artists, and writers.

Gertrude Stein (1935). *Courtesy of the Library of Congress, Prints & Photographs Division, Carl Van Vechten Collection, LC-USZ62-103680.*

POET, NOVELIST & PLAYWRIGHT

Born: Allegheny, Pennsylvania
Died: Neuilly-sur-Seine, France
Buried: Père Lachaise Cemetery, Paris, France

Gertrude Stein's apartment at 27 Rue de Fleurus in Paris, France.

Alice B. Toklas (1949). *Courtesy of the Library of Congress, Prints & Photographs Division, Carl Van Vechten Collection, LC-USZ62-42496.*

The famous salons held at her home during this period have become legendary and would help define modernist literature and art. Regular attendees included Pablo Picasso, Henri Matisse, Ernest Hemingway, F. Scott Fitzgerald, James Joyce, Ezra Pound, and many others. Alice B. Toklas became the informal hostess for the female guests who were segregated in another room during the gatherings. Stein credited the origins of these salons to Matisse, stating "more and more frequently, people began visiting to see the Matisse paintings and the Cézannes. Matisse brought people, everybody brought somebody, and they came at any time and it began to be a nuisance, and it was in this way that Saturday evenings began." Stein has also been credited with coining the term "Lost Generation," whose members came of age during and after World War I. This term was popularized by Ernest Hemingway in his novel, *The Sun Also Rises* (1926). In *A Moveable Feast* (1964), Hemingway revealed that the expression actually came from the owner of a car repair business who had serviced Stein's car. When a young mechanic botched the repair of Stein's car, she witnessed the garage owner berate the boy, "You are all a génération perdue" (a lost generation). Stein, in retelling the story to Hemingway, added, "That is what you are. That's what you all are...all of you young people who served in the war. You are a lost generation."

Stein would write the bulk of her literary works between 1903 and 1914, and her first significant novel, *Three Lives*, was published in 1909. This was followed by *The Making of Americans* (1925), the manuscript of which remained unpublished until 1924 when, on the advice of Ernest Hemingway, Stein agreed to publish excerpts in *The Transatlantic Review*. Her other works included *Tender Buttons* (1914), the best known of her "hermetic" works.

During the 1930s and 1940s, Stein concentrated on a variety of different writing genres, from memoir to art criticism. Works of this period include *How to Write* (1931) and *The Geographical History of America: The Relation of Human Nature to the Human Mind* (1936), which explained the basis of her literary practice and theory. In 1933, she published *The Autobiography of Alice B. Toklas*, which was disguised as an autobiography authored by Alice B. Toklas, but in reality was written by Stein. It was the first of her writings to be published in *The Atlantic Monthly*. She later admitted to writing it in six weeks with the sole purpose of making money. Many of her friends thought the book was too commercial; Hemingway called it "a damned pitiful book," but the financial rewards enabled Stein to live a more affluent lifestyle.

In 1934, Stein returned to the United States and began a very successful lecture tour. She then returned to France and wrote *Portraits and Prayers* (1934). This book was a collection of remembrances of her Paris friends and acquaintances. She then wrote a sequel to *The Autobiography of Alice B. Toklas,* entitled *Everybody's Autobiography* (1937), and *Picasso* (1939), a humorous and revealing study of the development of the great painter's art. During World War II and the German occupation of Paris, Stein lived in Culoz, France. She returned to Paris after the Allied liberation in 1944. Her reactions to the war were recorded in *Paris, France* (1940), *Wars I Have Seen* (1945), and *Brewsie and Willie* (1946), which was published a week before her death.

On July 27, 1946, Stein died from stomach cancer at her home in Neuilly-sur-Seine, France, and was buried at Père Lachaise Cemetery in Paris. She named writer and photographer Carl Van Vechten as her literary executor and he helped to posthumously publish many of her works, including *The Previously Uncollected Writings of Gertrude Stein* (1974) and *Dear Sammy: Letters from Gertrude Stein and Alice B. Toklas* (1977). Although Stein had bequeathed the majority of her estate to Toklas, including their shared art collection, the couple's relationship was not legally recognized by the courts. As the paintings appreciated in value, Stein's relatives took action to claim them, eventually removing them from Toklas' home. For the remainder of her life, Toklas relied on contributions from friends, as well as her own writing, to support herself. In 1954, she published a quirky memoir that was a mixture of memories and recipes under the title *The Alice B. Toklas Cookbook*. She also wrote articles for several magazines and newspapers. In 1963, she published her autobiography, *What Is Remembered,* which abruptly ends with Stein's death, leaving little uncertainty that Stein was the love of her life. In later years, she suffered from poor health and continued financial difficulties. Toklas died on March 7, 1967, and was buried beside Stein at Père Lachaise Cemetery.

Grave of Gertude Stein at Père Lachaise Cemetery in Paris, France.

Robert Frost
(1874–1963)

Robert Frost, photographed by Fred Palumbo in 1941. *Courtesy of the Library of Congress, Prints & Photographs Division, LC-USZ62-120742.*

POET

Born: San Francisco, California

Died: Boston, Massachusetts

Buried: Old Bennington Cemetery, Bennington, Vermont

"Two roads diverged in a wood and I took the one less traveled by, and that has made all the difference."

ROBERT FROST

Robert Frost was a conventional poet and, through the use of New England expressions, surroundings, and characters, he was able to brilliantly portray the roots of American culture. Although he never graduated from college, during his lifetime he received more than forty honorary degrees from prestigious institutions, such as Princeton, Oxford, and Cambridge. He was born Robert Lee Frost on March 26, 1874, in San Francisco, California, the son of William Prescott Frost Jr. and Isabella Moodie. When Frost's father, who was a noted journalist, died in 1884, his will requested that he be buried in his native New England. His widow and two children traveled east for the funeral, but, lacking funds to return to California, they decided to remain in Salem, Massachusetts. As a child, Robert lacked interest in school, but eventually became a serious student. In 1892, he briefly attended Dartmouth College, where he met his future wife, Elinor Miriam White. He quickly lost interest in academics and returned home. He found work at a variety of different jobs and began to write poetry. In 1894, his first poem, "My Butterfly," was published in *The New York Independent*. Overconfident because of these early accomplishments, he eagerly proposed marriage to Elinor, who refused, wanting to complete college before marriage. Depressed over her rejection, Frost went on an extended walking trip of the Great Dismal Swamp in Virginia. Upon his return, he again proposed to Elinor; this time she accepted and they were married on December 19, 1895, in Lawrence, Massachusetts. Together they would have six children.

In 1897, Frost began attending Harvard University, but college academics proved difficult and health issues forced him to withdraw after two years. Afterwards, Frost found work tending to his deceased grandfather's farm in Derry, New Hampshire. Frost would live and work on this farm for the next nine years. It was here that he wrote many of his most famous poems. Ultimately, farming proved unproductive and Frost turned to teaching. From 1906 to 1911, he taught at several private academies and colleges in the New Hampshire area.

Robert Frost's farm in Derry, New Hampshire.

Frost sold his Derry, New Hampshire, farm in 1912 and moved to England. He and Elinor settled in Buckinghamshire and he continued to write poetry. During this period, he met and befriended many intellectuals who helped inspire and further expand his command of poetry. In 1913, Frost published *A Boy's Will*; although this collection of poetry contained some antiquated language, the rhythms were simple and it was well-received. The following year, he published *North of Boston* (1914), which established him as one of the preeminent nature poets. His intention was not to venerate nature, but comment on its beauty and isolation.

When he returned to the United States in 1915, *North of Boston* was already a bestseller. He was by nature shy and reserved, and the sudden fame made him extremely uncomfortable. He withdrew to a small farm in Franconia, New Hampshire. Over time, he would overcome his shyness and develop a brief and simple speaking technique that made him one of the most admired lecturers of his day. In 1916, he published *Mountain Interval* and began teaching English at Amherst College. He would be one of the first poets-in-residence on an American college campus, and would hold various academic positions intermittently for the next twenty-five years. During this same period, he also taught at the University of Michigan and Harvard. He spent nearly every summer between 1921 and 1963 teaching at the Bread Loaf School of English at Middlebury College in Ripton, Vermont.

In 1924, Frost was awarded the first of four Pulitzer Prizes for *New Hampshire: A Poem with Notes and Grace Notes*. He would win additional awards for *Collected Poems* (1931), *A Further Range* (1937), and *A Witness Tree* (1943). In 1927, he purchased a five-acre estate in South Miami, Florida, where he would spend winters for the remainder of his life. The following year, he published *West Running Brook* and began traveling extensively. After his wife's death in 1938, he resigned his position at Amherst and accepted an offer from Harvard. He then wrote several books of poetry that included *Collected Poems* (1939) and *Complete Poems* (1949). In 1961, he was asked to speak at the inauguration of President John F. Kennedy. During the ceremony, he recited the poem "The Gift Outright." This was the first time a poet had spoken at a U.S. president's inauguration. The following year, he published his last collection of poems, *In the Clearing*. On January 29, 1963, Robert Frost died following complications from prostate surgery in Boston, Massachusetts. He was buried within the Frost family plot at the Old Bennington Cemetery in Bennington, Vermont, and the epitaph adorning his grave marker reads: "I had a lover's quarrel with the world."

Robert Frost's cabin in Ripton, Vermont.

ROBERT LEE FROST
MAR 26, 1874 — JAN 29, 1963
"I HAD A LOVERS QUARREL WITH THE WORLD"

HIS WIFE
ELINOR MIRIAM WHITE
OCT 25, 1873 — MAR 20, 1938
"TOGETHER WING TO WING AND OAR TO OAR"

MARJORIE FROST FRASER
MAR 29, 1905 — MAY 2, 1934

CAROL FROST
MAY 27, 1902 — OCT 9, 1940

ELLIOTT FROST
SEPT 28, 1896 — JULY 28, 1900

ELINOR BETTINA FROST
JUNE 20, 1907 — JUNE 21, 1907

LILLIAN LaBATT FROST
NOV 13, 1905 — DEC 19, 1995

Grave of poet Robert Frost at the Old Bennington Cemetery in Bennington, Vermont.

> "No one connected intimately with a writer has any appreciation of his temperament, except to think him overdoing everything."
>
> ZANE GREY

Zane Grey became one of the first millionaire authors and penned more than ninety novels. He became an inspiration for future generations of Western writers and was a major force in shaping many of the legends of the Old West. Critics have claimed that his depictions of the West are too fanciful and historically inaccurate to the realities of the frontier. Many of his novels would be adapted to film and television. Pearl Zane Gray (he would later change the spelling of his last name) was born on January 31, 1872, in Zanesville, Ohio, the son of Lewis Gray and Alice Josephine Zane. As a child, he was known for his quick temper and rebellious nature. He loved to read and often spent hours reading adventure stories and dime store novels. In 1889, the family moved to Columbus, Ohio, where Zane found work as a part-time usher in a movie theater and played summer baseball for a semi-pro team with hopes of one day becoming a major leaguer. He was a good hitter and pitcher, and was offered a scholarship to the University of Pennsylvania. Academically, Grey barely achieved passing grades and his shy nature set him apart from other students. He struggled with the dream of becoming either a writer or professional baseball player, but eventually concluded that dentistry would be the practical choice.

Zane Grey (from an undated photograph). *Courtesy of the Altadena Historical Society.*

In 1898, he graduated with a degree in dentistry and established a dental practice in New York City. In his spare time, he wrote to offset boredom and continued to play baseball with several minor league clubs, including the Newark Colts and the Orange Athletic Club. His brother, Romer "Reddy" Grey was also a ballplayer who briefly played with the Pittsburgh Pirates in 1903.

Zane Gray as a member of the University of Pennsylvania varsity baseball team in 1895.

NOVELIST

Born: Zanesville, Ohio

Died: Altadena, California

Buried: Union Cemetery, Lackawaxen, Pennsylvania

Zane Grey's home in Lackawaxen, Pennsylvania (undated photograph). *Courtesy of the Library of Congress, Prints & Photographs Division, HABS PA, 52-LACK, 36.*

He was also an avid fisherman who penned the book *Adventures of a Deep Sea Angler* (1930). Zane's love for baseball would later inspire him to write several sports related novels, such as *The Young Pitcher* (1911) and *The Redheaded Outfield and Other Baseball Stories* (1920).

With a love for nature and adventure, Zane often ventured out of the city with his brothers. They would travel to rural Pennsylvania on canoeing and fishing expeditions. It was on one of these trips that he would meet his future wife, Lina "Dolly" Roth. During their courtship, he told her that he intended to keep seeing other women, stating, "I love to be free. I cannot change my spots. The ordinary man is satisfied with a moderate income, a home, wife, children, and all that...but I am a million miles from being that kind of man and no amount of trying will ever do any good...I shall never lose the spirit of my interest in women." Despite this ominous beginning, they were married on November 21, 1905, and would have three children. Shortly after returning from their honeymoon to California, Zane impulsively decided to close his dental practice and move to Lackawaxen, Pennsylvania, where he planned to devote more time to writing adventure stories. During this period, he suffered episodes of severe depression, which affected him for most of his life. As he described it, "A hyena lying in ambush, that is my black spell. I conquered one mood only to fall prey to the next...I wandered about like a lost soul or a man who was conscious of imminent death." In writing, Grey would find respite from the harsh realities of life and his inner demons.

In 1906, he published *Spirit of the Border*, which described the adventures of brothers who take different life paths upon their arrival to the Ohio River Valley during the late 18th century. This novel was the second in a trilogy, the first of which, *Betty Zane* (1903), was self-published and the third, *The Last Trail*, was published in 1909. In the coming years, he published many novels, including *The Last of the Plainsmen* (1908), *The Heritage of the Desert* (1910), *Riders of the Purple Sage* (1912), and *The Rainbow Trail* (1915). Grey often spent months away from his family fishing, writing, and spending time with his many mistresses. While his wife was aware of his behavior, she seemed to view it as a handicap, rather than a choice. Throughout their life together, Zane would highly value her management of his literary career and their family. In addition to her considerable editorial skills, she had good business sense and handled all his contract negotiations.

In 1918, Grey moved to California, and settled in Altadena. He summed up his feelings for the area stating: "In Altadena, I have found those qualities that make life worth living." It was there that he established Zane Grey Productions, a film company that would later become Paramount Pictures. During this same period, he met Brenda Montenegro, with whom he would carry on a torrid love affair. The two met while hiking in Eaton Canyon and Zane wrote, "I saw her flowing raven mane against the rocks of the canyon. I have seen the red skin of the Navajo and the olive of the Spaniards, but her skin looked as if her creator had in that instant molded her just for me. I thought it was an apparition. She seemed to be the embodiment of the West I portray in my books, open and wild."

Between 1925 and his death in 1939, Grey spent more and more time away from home and traveled extensively to the South Pacific, New Zealand, and Australia. The financial turmoil caused by the Great Depression had a very limited impact on his literary career. Unlike many writers, who could effectively write every day, Zane would often suffer from long periods of writer's block and then have sudden bursts of creativity that resulted in endless hours of writing. Near the end of his life, he had a fatalistic view of the future and wrote: "The so-called civilization of man and his works shall perish from the earth, while the shifting sands, the red looming walls, the purple sage, and the towering monuments, the vast brooding range show no perceptible change." On October 23, 1939, Zane Grey died from a heart attack at his home in Altadena, California. He was buried at the Union Cemetery in Lackawaxen, Pennsylvania.

ZANE GREY
1872 — 1939
LINA ELISE GREY
1883 — 1957

1– Zane Grey Estate in Altadena, California. Grey died here on October 23, 1939.

2– Grave of Zane Grey at the Union Cemetery in Lackawaxen, Pennsylvania. *Courtesy of Jane Butler © 2012.*

Edgar Rice Burroughs
(1875–1950)

Edgar Rice Burroughs (1934).
Courtesy of Edgar Rice Burroughs Incorporated.

NOVELIST & SHORT STORY WRITER

Born: Chicago, Illinois

Died: Encino, California

Buried: Edgar Rice Burroughs Inc. Office Building

Tarzana, California

"I write to escape; to escape poverty."
EDGAR RICE BURROUGHS

Edgar Rice Burroughs was the creator of Tarzan, one of the legendary icons of popular culture. He also wrote numerous science fiction, adventure, and crime novels, as well as many short stories for popular pulp fiction magazines. He was born on September 1, 1875, in Chicago, Illinois, the son of George Tyler Burroughs and Mary Evaline Zieger. His early education was inconsistent, and he was transferred from school to school. In 1891, Edgar was sent to live with his older brothers in Idaho because of an influenza outbreak in Chicago. The six months he spent on the frontier were some of the happiest of his childhood. He was then sent to the Phillips Academy in Andover, Massachusetts, and the Michigan Military Academy at Orchard Lake. At the latter, he began to excel at academics and horseback riding. After graduating from the academy in 1895, he tried, and failed, to gain entrance to the U.S. Military Academy at West Point. Unconcerned, he then enlisted in the regular army, where he was assigned to the 7th U.S. Cavalry regiment at Fort Grant in the Arizona territory. Two years later, he was medically discharged because of a heart condition.

After leaving the army, Burroughs spent several months drifting throughout the West before returning home to Chicago to work for his father at the American Battery Company. In January 1900, he married Emma Hulbert, a childhood friend, and together they would have three children. Over the next few years, Burroughs drifted from job to job without any purpose before turning to writing. According to his official biography, the turning point came after he had read several pulp fiction magazines. Burroughs later wrote, "If people were paid for writing rot such as I read in some of those magazines…I could write stories just as rotten. Although I had never written a story, I knew absolutely that I could write stories just as entertaining and probably a whole lot more so than any I chanced to read in those magazines." In 1911, Burroughs began writing full-time. His first novel, *Under the Moons of Mars*, which introduced the character John Carter, was first serialized in *All-Story Magazine*. Six years later, it was published in book form and re-titled *A Princess of Mars*.

Edgar Rice Burroughs,
A Princess of Mars;
cover art by Frank E.
Schoonover, 1917.

In October 1912, Burroughs' most famous work, *Tarzan of the Apes*, was serialized in *All-Story Magazine*. It tells the tale of a young boy who is adopted by apes after the death of his parents. The novel was published in book form in 1914. The Tarzan series was a financial success, and Burroughs was determined to capitalize on its popularity in every way possible. He soon began to diversify the Tarzan brand through numerous media outlets; his efforts led to sequels, comic strips, movies, and merchandise. Eventually, there would be a total of twenty-six *Tarzan* novels.

Over his literary lifetime, Burroughs would write over seventy novels, including *The Land That Time Forgot* (1918), *The Cave Girl* (1925), *The War Chief* (1927), and *Apache Devil* (1933). In 1919, he moved to Southern California and purchased a large tract of land in the San Fernando Valley, north of Los Angeles, which he named Tarzana. It was there that he founded his own publishing house, Edgar Rice Burroughs, Incorporated. In his later years, his literary acclaim and financial success were overshadowed by personal issues, including a divorce from his first wife in 1934. The following year, he married former silent film actress Florence Gilbert. She was the ex-wife of Ashton Dearholt, with whom Burroughs had co-founded the Burroughs-Tarzan Enterprises film production company.

In 1940, Burroughs moved to Hawaii and continued to write. After the bombing of Pearl Harbor, he volunteered to become a war correspondent and reported on troop activities in the Pacific theater. In 1942, Florence filed for divorce, citing Burroughs' verbal abuse and heavy drinking as factors in the marriage's demise. After the war, he returned to California and continued to write. On March 19, 1950, he died from a heart attack at his Encino home. His ashes were scattered beneath a mulberry tree in the courtyard of the Edgar Rice Burroughs office building in Tarzana, California.

The Edgar Rice Burroughs Office Building in Tarzana, California.

Jack London
(1876–1916)

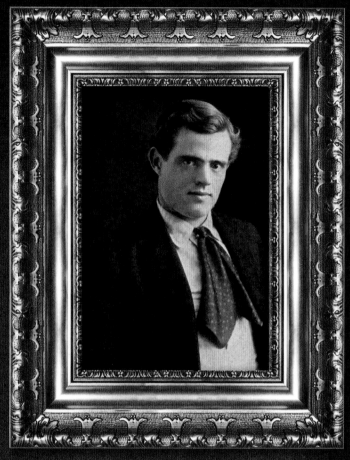

Jack London, circa 1903.

NOVELIST & SHORT STORY WRITER

Born: San Francisco, California

Died: Glen Ellen, Sonoma County, California

Buried: Jack London State Historic Park

Glen Ellen, California

"I write for no other purpose than to add to the beauty that now belongs to me. I write a book for no other reason than to add three or four hundred acres to my magnificent estate."

JACK LONDON

Jack London was one of the first successful writers of commercial magazine fiction and was an outspoken supporter of unionization and socialism. He was born John Griffith Chaney on January 12, 1876, in San Francisco, the child of famed astrologer William Chaney and Flora Wellman. Whether Wellman and Chaney were ever legally married is not known. According to Wellman, upon discovering that she was pregnant, Chaney demanded that she have an abortion. When she refused, he disavowed paternity of his child and refused to provide any financial support.

In late 1876, Flora Wellman married John London, and they moved to Oakland, California. While the London family suffered some financial distress, they were not as poor as London's later accounts claimed. As a teenager, Jack had little interest in school and dreamed of adventure. He decided to quit school, and found employment pirating oysters on San Francisco Bay and sailing the Pacific. He even joined Kelly's Army of unemployed working men! After returning home at age 19, he finished high school. During these journeys, he became an enthusiastic supporter of

Flora Wellman, Jack London's mother (1921) from The Book of Jack London (1921) by Charmian London.

socialist doctrine, and soon became known as the Boy Socialist of Oakland for his public speaking. He deliberately chose to become a writer to escape what he perceived to be the dreadful prospects and ordinary life of a factory worker. He began studying the writing styles of prominent authors and started submitting short stories and poems to various magazines, with limited success.

London began attending the University of California, Berkeley, in 1896, but financial circumstances forced him to withdraw from school a year later. He then traveled to the Alaskan Gold Fields in search of fame and fortune. After spending the winter of 1897 in the Yukon Territory, he began to write about his experiences, publishing several stories in the *Overland Monthly*. In the coming years, he would produce over fifty works that included short stories, novels, and political essays. His most famous novel, *The Call of the Wild*, was published in 1903, and he followed its success with a scathing critique of capitalism in *The People of the Abyss* (1903). In 1907, he began a long voyage through the South Pacific. Through writing about these experiences, he popularized Polynesian culture and Hawaii as a tourist destination.

London was one of the most widely read and popular writers of his day, and he used this platform to promote political issues, such as Socialism, women's suffrage, and prohibition. He was one of the first writers to work with the film industry, and saw a number of his novels made into films. His novel *The Sea-Wolf* (1904) became the basis for one of the first full-length American movies. He was also one of the first authors to endorse commercial products in advertising. His ideology often lacked consistency. For example, he supported women's suffrage and created some of the

Charmian Kittredge, second wife of Jack London, circa 1905. *Courtesy of the Library of Congress, Prints & Photographs Division, George G. Bain Collection, LC-DIG-GGBAIN-05364.*

most independent and strong-willed female characters in American literature, yet in his personal life, he was domineering and heavy-handed towards his wives and daughters. His Socialist ideals were passionate, but were countered by a strong drive toward individualism and capitalist success. These contradictory themes have made him a difficult figure to reduce to simple terms.

In 1900, London married Bessie Maddern, with whom he would have two daughters. The couple both publicly acknowledged that they were not marrying out of love, but because of friendship and a belief that they would produce strong offspring. London made it clear that he did not love Bessie, but that he liked her well enough to attempt a successful marriage. In choosing her, London followed the principles of a book he had co-authored with Anna Strunsky, *The Kempton-Wace Letters* (1903), in which he wrote that mates should be selected for good breeding, not love. Throughout their brief, three-year marriage, London often complained to friends about Bessie's penchant for chastity. On July 24, 1903, he left the marriage and was granted a divorce the following year. In 1905, he married what he termed his ideal "mate woman," Charmian Kittredge. London had been introduced to her in 1900 by George Platt Brett; Kittredge was Brett's secretary at MacMillan Publishing. In her, London found the embodiment of what he perceived to be the perfect woman and used her as a model for many of his future

female characters. She enthusiastically joined him on his travels and, with his encouragement, she wrote several books about their life together.

In 1905, London purchased a large tract of land in Sonoma County, California, which he named the Wolf House estate. He would later write that next to his wife, the ranch was the dearest thing in the world to him. After 1910, his literary works were

The Old Winery Cottage, Glen Ellen, California, where Jack London died on November 22, 1916.

Gravesite of Jack London at the Jack London State Historic Park in Glen Ellen, California.

mostly written out of financial necessity to provide an operating income for the estate. London successfully imported agricultural techniques that he had observed in Japan, and was ahead of his time in conceiving a ranch that was both self-sufficient and regenerating.

Throughout much of his adult life, London was troubled with numerous health issues that were compounded by his alcoholism. He died at his ranch on November 22, 1916, at the age of 39, from kidney failure. At the time of his death, he was in extreme pain and taking excessive amounts of morphine. It has been alleged that an overdose, either by accident or by design, may have contributed to his death. In his will, London left nearly his entire estate to his second wife, leaving only token amounts to his children. His ashes were scattered beneath a large boulder at the Jack London State Historic Park in Glen Ellen, California.

"The secret of happiness is to admire without desiring."

CARL SANDBURG

Carl Sandburg
(1878–1967)

Carl Sandburg (1955). *Courtesy of the Library of Congress, Prints & Photographs Division, LC-USZ62-115064.*

POET, BIOGRAPHER & CHILDREN'S AUTHOR

Born: Galesburg, Illinois

Died: Flat Rock, North Carolina

Buried: The Carl Sandburg Home National Historic Site
Galesburg, Illinois

Carl August Sandburg was awarded three Pulitzer Prizes: two for his poetry and another for his biography of Abraham Lincoln. He was born on January 6, 1878, in Galesburg, Illinois, the son of August Sandburg and Clara Mathilda Anderson. At the age of six, he decided that he wanted to be a writer. In 1898, at the outbreak of the Spanish American War, Sandburg enlisted in the army and was stationed in Puerto Rico with the 6th Illinois Infantry. Following the war, he briefly attended West Point, but his poor

Carl Sandburg's birthplace, Galesburg, Illinois.

academic performance forced him to withdraw. He returned to Galesburg and attended Lombard College (now Knox College), and began to write poetry.

In 1903, Sandburg decided to quit school and focus his attention on writing. He moved to Chicago, where he wrote for several minor journals and tried his hand at lecturing. His was successful and spoke on a variety of subjects, including the poetry of Walt Whitman, the politics of Abraham Lincoln, and the doctrines of Socialism. His firebrand style of oratory soon gained the attention of Wisconsin Social-Democratic party leader Winfield P. Gaylord, who asked Sandburg to become a party organizer. Sandburg accepted the position and began his assignment on December 29, 1907. On that same day, party member Lilian Steichen, the younger sister of photographer Edward Steichen, had stopped by to say hello to some friends and met, by chance, the new party organizer. She and Sandburg hit it off immediately and she gave him her address; he promised to write every day. Six months later, they were married in Milwaukee. Together, they would have three children.

In 1910, Sandburg served as secretary to Emil Seidel, the first Socialist Mayor of Milwaukee, and in his spare time wrote poetry. An ardent supporter of social justice, Sandburg eventually became disillusioned with Social-Democratic party politics and moved his family to Chicago, where he went to work at the *Chicago Evening World*. He also had several poems published.

Connemara, Carl Sandburg's rural estate in Flat Rock, North Carolina, where he lived from 1945 until his death in 1967.

In the coming years, his poetry became very popular, and this newfound fame allowed him to publish several compilations, such as *Chicago Poems* (1916), *Cornhuskers* (1918), for which he won his first Pulitzer Prize, *Smoke and Steel* (1920), and *Slabs of the Sunburnt West* (1922). In 1926, he began writing his biography of Abraham Lincoln. He completed the first two-volume set, *Abraham Lincoln: The Prairie Years*, the same year. For the next thirteen years, he wrote the four-volume sequel, *Abraham Lincoln: The War Years*, which dominated his creative life until its completion. In 1939, he was awarded a Pulitzer Prize in history for this work. His other works include *Remembrance Rock* (1948), *Complete Poems* (1950) for which he won a third Pulitzer Prize, *Harvest Poems, 1910–1960* (1960), and *Honey and Salt* (1963). He won a Grammy Award in 1959 for his recording of Aaron Copland's *Lincoln Portrait* with the New York Philharmonic.

Sandburg was a devoted father to his children and, to entertain them, he often made up fanciful fairy tales. He decided to publish these stories in book form after his eldest daughter was diagnosed with epilepsy. These stories include *Rootabaga Stories* (1922), *Rootabaga Pigeons* (1923), *Rootabaga Country* (1929), and *Potato Face* (1930). Sandburg also wrote two books of poems for children: *Early Moon* (1930) and *Wind Song* (1960).

In 1945, Sandburg moved to a rural farm in North Carolina, where he found the solitude he required for writing. He would spend the remaining years of his life on this farm, where he would publish more than a third of his works. In 1959, he gave a Lincoln Day address before a joint session of Congress before traveling on a State Department tour of the Soviet Union. He lived in Hollywood during much of 1960, working as George Stevens' creative consultant on *The Greatest Story Ever Told*. He published his last book of poetry, *Honey and Salt*, in 1963. The next year he received the Presidential Medal of Freedom. In the last years of his life, he was especially proud of the fact that more than half a dozen public schools had been named in his honor. Carl Sandburg died on July 22, 1967, from a heart attack at his home in North Carolina. His ashes were returned to his Galesburg, Illinois, birthplace and buried beneath a red granite boulder, named "Remembrance Rock." Upon her death in 1977, his wife's ashes were interred with those of her husband.

Carl Sandburg's ashes are interred beneath Remembrance Rock at his birthplace in Galesburg, Illinois.

"Every compulsion is put upon writers to become safe, polite, obedient, and sterile."

SINCLAIR LEWIS

Although Sinclair Lewis' novels were written during the 1920s, 1930s, and 1940s, they are still relevant today because of their unique imagery and descriptions of social institutions. William Shirer, a noted journalist and friend of Lewis, summed up Lewis' literary career, "It has become rather commonplace for so-called literary critics to write off Sinclair Lewis as a novelist. Compared to Fitzgerald, Hemingway, Dos Passos, and Faulkner, Lewis lacked style. Yet his impact on modern American life was greater than all of these four writers together."

Harry Sinclair Lewis was born on February 7, 1885, in Sauk Centre, Minnesota, the child of Edwin J. Lewis, M.D. and Emma Kermott. His father was very strict and had difficulty relating to his shy and sensitive son. Very little is known about his mother; she died in 1891 when Sinclair was only 6 years old. His father remarried the following year, and Sinclair apparently had a good relationship with his stepmother. Lewis' childhood diaries suggest that he was a serious student, but because of his shy nature, had difficulty making friends. At age 13, he ran away from home and unsuccessfully tried to join the army.

Lewis began to write while in high school and some of his stories were published in the local newspaper. In 1902, Lewis began attending Oberlin Academy in hopes of qualifying for acceptance to Yale University. The next year, he was accepted at Yale, where many of his early works appeared in the *Yale Courant* and *The Yale Literary Magazine*, for which he became an editor. Lewis interrupted his education in 1907 to work briefly at Helicon Hall, a New Jersey utopian colony created by writer Upton Sinclair. The colony

Boyhood home of Sinclair Lewis in Sauk Centre, Minnesota. *Courtesy of Sally E. Parry, Sinclair Lewis Society.*

Sinclair Lewis
(1885–1951)

Sinclair Lewis circa 1914. *Courtesy of the Library of Congress, Prints & Photographs Division, LC-USZ62-52462.*

NOVELIST

Born: Sauk Centre, Minnesota

Died: Rome, Italy

Buried: Greenwood Cemetery, Sauk Centre, Minnesota

included artists, writers, sculptors, and painters who all worked together. Contrary to popular belief, the colony had very little to do with politics. He graduated from Yale in 1908, after which he wrote for several newspapers and publishing houses. During this period, he wrote numerous articles and short stories that were published in a variety of magazines. Many of these works showed early signs of the satiric skill that would be evident in his later novels. He also sold several story plots to novelist Jack London. In 1914, Lewis married Grace Livingston Hegger, an editor at *Vogue* magazine. In 1928, they divorced, and Lewis married Dorothy Thompson, a political columnist. Lewis and Thompson would divorce in 1942.

Lewis wrote and published his first novel, *Hike and the Aeroplane*, in 1912 under the pseudonym Tom Graham. His next works were *Our Mr. Wrenn* (1914), *The Trail of the Hawk* (1915), and *The Job* (1917). In 1920, Lewis would achieve great success with the publication of *Main Street*, the story of an imaginative but immature young woman who marries a doctor in an attempt to improve her lifestyle. The conflict between the doctor and the young woman's vision of the future makes up the novel's central plot line. Lewis followed this success with the controversial bestselling novel *Babbitt* (1922). The book is a satire of American culture, which harshly criticized middle-class America and its lack of individuality.

In 1925, Lewis published *Arrowsmith*, in which he returned to the style of *Main Street* to portray a young doctor's battle to maintain his ethics in a dishonest world. The novel is still required reading in many medical schools. He was awarded the Pulitzer Prize for the novel, but turned down the honor because the terms of the award required that it be given not for a work of value, but for a work that presents "the wholesome atmosphere of American life." His next novel, *Elmer Gantry* (1927), with its theme of religious hypocrisy, was denounced by many religious leaders and banned in some U.S. cities.

In 1930, Lewis became the first American author to win the Nobel Prize for literature. In his acceptance speech, he praised fellow writers Theodore Dreiser, Willa Cather, and Ernest Hemingway, but also lamented that: "In America, most of us, not readers alone, but even writers, are still afraid of any literature which is not a glorification of everything American, a glorification of our faults as well as our virtues, and that America is the most contradictory, the most depressing, the most stirring, of any land in the world today." He also offered a philosophical criticism of the American literary establishment: "Our American professors like their literature clear and cold and pure and very dead."

Throughout his entire adult life, Lewis suffered from bouts of alcoholism. In 1937, after a night of binge drinking, he checked himself into a psychiatric hospital in Stockbridge, Massachusetts, but left after only ten days. One of his treating doctors later wrote that Lewis lacked any fundamental understanding of his problem. In the coming years, he wrote eleven more novels, which included *Cass Timberlane* (1945), *Kingsblood Royal* (1947), and *The God-Seeker* (1949). He spent the last years of his life living in Europe, keenly aware that his impact on American literature was far less than his early admirers had led him to believe. Due to health issues, he became semi-reclusive. Lewis died on January 10, 1951, from a heart attack (caused by advanced alcoholism) at a small town hospital outside of Rome, Italy. His remains were cremated and returned to the United States for burial at Greenwood Cemetery in Sauk Centre, Minnesota.

Grave of Sinclair Lewis at Greenwood Cemetery, Sauk Centre, Minnesota. *Courtesy of Sally E. Parry, Sinclair Lewis Society.*

> *"Life is for each man a solitary cell*
> *whose walls are mirrors."*

EUGENE O'NEILL
from Lazarus Laughed

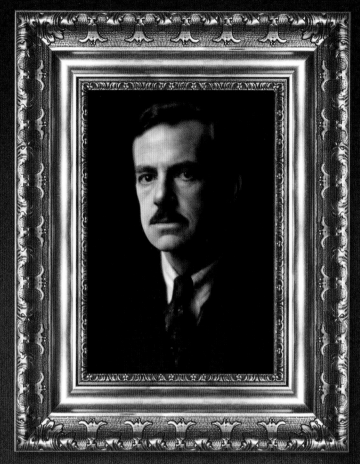

Eugene O'Neill by Alice Boughton. *Courtesy of the Library of Congress, Prints & Photographs Division, LC-B7901-36.*

PLAYWRIGHT

Born: New York City

Died: Boston, Massachusetts,

Buried: Forest Hills Cemetery, Boston, Massachusetts

Eugene O'Neill was one of the most popular playwrights of the 20th century, and four of his plays were honored with Pulitzer Prizes. He was also awarded a Nobel Prize for literature in 1936. He was born on October 16, 1888, at the Barrett Hotel in New York City, the child of Irish actor James O'Neill and Mary Ellen Quinlan. Eugene spent most of his early childhood touring the country with his father. This itinerant lifestyle, coupled with his mother's drug addiction, had a profound impact on him.

O'Neill was eventually sent to a Catholic boarding school, where he rebelled against the strict atmosphere. He attended Princeton University for one year, and historians have speculated that he might have been kicked out due to poor attendance, or for conduct violations, such as an incident in which he was accused of throwing a bottle through the classroom window of future U.S. President Woodrow Wilson, who was then a professor at the school. O'Neill also suffered numerous bouts of depression and was a heavy drinker, which may have also led to his withdrawal or dismissal from school. Either way, he left school and began to travel.

On October 2, 1909, he married Kathleen Jenkins. They would have one child together. Their marriage ended in divorce three years later, and O'Neill was so depressed at its failure that he attempted suicide. He recovered only to discover that he had contracted tuberculosis. While recuperating, he made the fateful decision to become a playwright. His father agreed to provide him with a small allowance and, in the fall of 1914, O'Neill briefly attended a drama technique course at Harvard University, but failed to complete the class. He then moved to Greenwich Village, where he became a member of the literary scene. During this time, he became close friends with John Reed, who was a successful journalist and socialist activist. Reed helped O'Neill get some of his early works published. In June 1916, Reed went to see a doctor about some health issues and was told that he needed an operation to remove a kidney. While Reed was recuperating, O'Neill began an affair with his wife, Louise Bryant. The affair was an open secret among their circle of friends, although Reed remained unaware. On July 28, 1916, O'Neill's first play *Bound East for Cardiff* was performed at the Provincetown Theater in Provincetown, Massachusetts.

"Spithead" in Warwick, Bermuda. The home of Eugene O'Neill and his wife, Agnes Bougton, from 1918-1929.

Eugene O'Neill and Carlotta Monterey (1933). *Courtesy of the Library of Congress, Prints & Photographs Division, Carl Van Vechten Collection, LC-USZ62-42540.*

Grave of Eugene O'Neill at Forest Hills Cemetery in Boston.

In 1917, O'Neill met Agnes Boulton, a successful writer; they married on April 12, 1918, and would have two children together. During this same period, he continued to suffer from bouts of depression, compounded by the deaths of his parents and older brother. Over the next three years, he wrote ten plays, including *The Sniper* (1917), *In the Zone* (1917), *The Long Voyage Home* (1917), *Moon of the Caribbees* (1918), *Shell-Shock* (1918), and *The Emperor Jones* (1920), all of which were performed at the Provincetown Theater. O'Neill initially concentrated on writing one-act plays, but it was his first full-length drama, *Beyond the Horizon* (1920), that established his reputation. This play won a Pulitzer Prize and was followed by *Anna Christie* (1921), *The Hairy Ape* (1922), *Desire Under the Elms* (1924), *All God's Chillun Got Wings* (1924), *The Great God Brown* (1926), and *Strange Interlude* (1928).

In 1929, O'Neill left his wife and began a relationship with actress Carlotta Monterey. Two months after his divorce was finalized, he married Monterey and moved to France. During their first years together, Monterey organized O'Neill's personal life, enabling him to devote himself to writing. The couple would separate numerous times during their relationship, but never divorced. In the early 1930s, O'Neill returned to the United States and eventually settled in Danville, California. Suffering from alcoholism, depression, and diagnosed with Parkinson's disease, O'Neill's health began to steadily decline during this period. His literary output was limited as well, although, in 1936, he was awarded the Nobel Prize for literature.

In 1940, he wrote a semi-autobiographical play titled *Long Day's Journey Into Night*, the action of which takes place during a single day in August 1912 at the summer home of the Tyrone family. O'Neill left specific instructions that the play was not to be made public until twenty-five years after his death. When *The Iceman Cometh* was released in 1946, it was his first new play in twelve years. One of his favorite plays, O'Neill claimed the drama was an attempt to portray man as a "victim of the ironies of life and himself."

O'Neill had strained relationships with all of his children. After his daughter, Oona, married actor Charlie Chaplin in 1943, he never spoke to her again. He was also estranged from his son, Shane, who later committed suicide. Eugene O'Neill Jr., much like his father, suffered from alcoholism and depression and, in 1950, would also commit suicide. On November 27, 1953, Eugene O'Neill died at the Sheraton Hotel on Bay State Road in Boston, Massachusetts. As he lay dying, he is alleged to have whispered: "I knew it. I knew it. Born in a hotel room and died in a hotel room." The building was later purchased by Boston University and became the Shelton Hall dormitory. He was buried at Forest Hills Cemetery in Boston. A later investigation of his autopsy records revealed that he did not actually suffer from Parkinson's disease. Despite his express wishes that *Long Day's Journey into Night* not be released to the public until twenty-five years after his death, his estate allowed it to be performed in 1956, and the following year it was awarded a Pulitzer Prize.

"The secret of joy in work is contained in one word – excellence. To know how to do something well is to enjoy it."

PEARL S. BUCK

Pearl S. Buck, circa 1932. *Courtesy of the Library of Congress, Prints & Photographs Division, LC-USZ62-10297.*

NOVELIST, PLAYWRIGHT & ESSAYIST

Born: Hillsboro, West Virginia

Died: Danby, Vermont

Buried: Green Hills Farm grounds, Perkasie, Pennsylvania

Pearl S. Buck was the first woman to win a Nobel Prize in literature. She often used personal experiences and political views as subject matter for her novels. These topics included women's rights, Asian culture, immigration, adoption, missionary work, and war. She has more than 100 written works to her credit, but even more significant, perhaps, are the 300-plus awards she received for humanitarian efforts on behalf of improved race relations worldwide.

The Stulting House at Pearl S. Buck's birthplace in Hillsboro, West Virginia.

She was born Pearl Sydenstricker on June 26, 1892, in Hillsboro, West Virginia, the daughter of Absalom Sydenstricker and Caroline Stulting. Her parents were Presbyterian missionaries stationed in China. Her family had returned to the United States shortly before her birth because of the deaths of several other children. Despite these tragedies, they chose to return to China when Pearl was three months old. There, Pearl learned to speak fluent Chinese. In 1911, she left China to attend Randolph-Macon Woman's College in Lynchburg, Virginia, and three years later was awarded a bachelor's degree. Following graduation, she accepted a teaching position at the college, but had to return to China to care for her sick mother. In 1917, she met and married John Lossing Buck, an American agricultural specialist. The couple settled in northern China. From 1921 until 1934, the Bucks lived in Nanking where he taught agricultural theory and she occasionally taught English literature. In 1925, Pearl

Green Hills Farm, Pearl S. Buck's country home in Perkasie, Pennsylvania.

Grave of Pearl S. Buck on the grounds of Green Hills Farm, Perkasie, Pennsylvania.

returned to the United States and began attending Cornell University in pursuit of a Master's degree in English. After graduating in 1926, she returned to China and began to write.

In 1930, she published her first novel, *East Wind: West Wind*, which discussed the conflict between the old and modern traditions in China. The book was the first in a trilogy of novels that would include *Sons* (1932) and *A House Divided* (1935). In 1933, she received a second Master's degree, this time from Yale University, and the following year decided to permanently stay in the United States. She divorced John Buck in 1935 and then married her publisher, Richard J. Walsh. In 1938, Buck was the first woman to be awarded the Nobel Prize for literature.

Over the next three decades, Buck continued to write, but she also worked tirelessly to promote racial tolerance and ease the struggles of underprivileged Asians, particularly children. In 1941, she founded the East and West Association to promote greater understanding among the people of the world. Eight years later, she established Welcome House, an adoption agency for Asian-American children. A dedicated supporter of multi-racial families, in the early 1960s she organized the Pearl S. Buck Foundation, which supported Asian-American children and their mothers living abroad. Although Buck's literary career embraced a variety of topics, almost all of her novels are set in China, including *Dragon Seed* (1942), *The Promise* (1943), *Peony* (1948), *Letter from Peking* (1957), *The Living Reed* (1963), and *The New Year* (1968). In the late 1940s, Buck wrote four novels under the pen name John Sedges: *The Angry Wife* (1947), *The Long Love* (1949), *Voices in the House* (1953), and *The Townsman* (1958). She also wrote a play, *A Desert Incident*, which was produced in 1959. She was also a brilliant essayist, as seen in her "American Argument" (1949) and "Friend to Friend" (1958), which was an open and honest conversation with Philippine President Carlos P. Rómulo. She died from lung cancer on March 6, 1973, in Danby, Vermont, and was buried on the grounds of her home in Perkasie, Pennsylvania. She designed her own tombstone, which is inscribed with Chinese characters that represent her name, Pearl Sydenstricker.

"Knowledge is a polite word for dead but not buried imagination."

E.E. CUMMINGS

Poet E.E. Cummings' innovative style of writing caused many of his early works to be rejected and, for several decades, he was forced to self-publish. Literary critics often revealed a lack of understanding of his unorthodox techniques. His poetry often expressed a veneration of nature and also stressed the importance of individuality and reality. Edward Estlin Cummings was born on October 14, 1894, in Cambridge, Massachusetts, the child of Edward Cummings, a Harvard University professor and minister of the Old South Church in Boston, and Rebecca Haswell Clarke. Born into a Unitarian family, Cummings' early childhood was filled with a variety of learning experiences. He also became acquainted with many of New England's famous intellectuals and philosophers, such as William James and Josiah Royce. He knew from an early age that he wanted to become a writer.

In 1911, Cummings began attending Harvard University, where he developed an interest in modern poetry, which tended to ignore conventional styles. Several of his poems were published in the *Harvard Advocate*. He graduated magna cum laude in 1915 and delivered a controversial commencement address in which he remarked about popular poet Amy Lowell's many abnormalities. The following year he received a Master's degree in English and Classical Studies.

In 1917, Cummings enlisted in the Ambulance Corps with his friend and future novelist, John Dos Passos, but because of paperwork confusion, Cummings was not initially assigned to a unit. He then spent several weeks exploring Paris. During this same time, he was writing letters home that drew the attention of military censors. These letters openly expressed anti-war attitudes and a lack of hatred for the Germans. On September 21, 1917, Cummings, along with William Slater Brown (another future novelist), were arrested by French authorities on charges of espionage. They were held for three months in a military detention camp in Normandy. Cummings was released three months later, after his politically connected father intervened on his behalf. He would later use these experiences as the basis for his novel *The Enormous Room* (1922). Shortly after his return to the United States, Cummings was drafted into the army and served in the 73rd Infantry Division until the end of the war.

E.E. Cummings
(1894–1962)

Photograph of E.E. Cummings, circa 1953. *Courtesy of the Library of Congress, Prints & Photographs Division, LC-USZ62-113649.*

POET, NOVELIST & PLAYWRIGHT

Born: Cambridge, Massachusetts

Died: North Conway, New Hampshire

Buried: Forest Hills Cemetery, Boston, Massachusetts

Grave of E.E. Cummings at Forest Hills Cemetery in Boston, Massachusetts.

In 1921, he returned to Paris and began to write. His first collection of poetry, *Tulips and Chimneys,* was published in 1923. His next collection of poetry, *XLI Poems,* was published in 1925, which cemented his reputation as one of the great poets of the first half of the 20th century. The following year, his parents were involved in an auto accident, in which his father was killed and his mother was seriously injured. This incident would have a profound impact on Cummings, and his writing began to take on a darker tone. During the 1930s, he began to feel more and more separated from normal society and tended to write many versions of essentially the same poem.

Cummings married twice. His first marriage, in 1924, to Elaine Orr ended in divorce after less than a year. She had been the wife of one of Cummings' college friends, and they had carried on an affair prior to marriage. Their short union produced a daughter and under the terms of the divorce settlement, he was granted visitation rights, but Elaine refused to follow the agreement. As a result, Cummings did not see his daughter again for over 20 years. He married Anne Barton in 1929; they separated three years later and officially divorced in 1934. The year they separated, Cummings met Marion Morehouse, a fashion model and photographer. It is not clear whether the two were ever legally married, but Morehouse and Cummings would live together for the remainder of his life.

Cummings always considered himself a failure as a poet, but after 1945, a new generation of readers began to rediscover his writings. In 1950, he was awarded a fellowship by the Academy of American Poets, and Harvard University asked him to deliver the Charles Eliot Norton Lectures in 1952–1953. In 1954, he published *Poems, 1923–1954,* which was well received by critics. Despite his avant-garde writing style, much of his poetry is considered quite traditional. His writings often dealt with themes of love and nature, as well as the relationship of the individual to the world. His work showed a particular quirkiness with grammar, in which he arranged words into larger phrases and sentences. He was influenced by notable writers, such as Gertrude Stein and Ezra Pound, as well as the early poetry of Amy Lowell. His finest single volume of poetry is often considered to be *95 Poems* (1958), which was followed by *Collected Poems* (1960). His final collection of poetry, *73 Poems,* was published in 1963. In addition to these works, he also wrote several plays, a ballet, and fifteen other volumes of poetry. Cummings died from a stroke on September 3, 1962, at the Memorial Hospital in North Conway, New Hampshire, and his ashes were interred at Forest Hills Cemetery in Boston. Shortly before his death, he wrote the text for Marion Morehouse's book of photography entitled *Adventures in Value* (1962).

> *"All good writing is swimming under water and holding your breath."*
>
> F. SCOTT FITZGERALD

F. Scott Fitzgerald was one of the most celebrated literary figures of the 1920s and his works have inspired generations of writers. He was an extremely perceptive writer, whose real life was a study in contrasts. He was quite insecure about his literary accomplishments and viewed himself a failure. It was written in a *New York Times* editorial after his death that Fitzgerald "was better than he knew, for in fact and in the literary sense he invented a generation...He might have interpreted them and even guided them, as in their middle years they saw a different and nobler freedom threatened with destruction." Into the 21st century, millions of copies of *The Great Gatsby* have been sold worldwide, and the novel is required reading in many high school and college classes.

He was born Francis Scott Key Fitzgerald on September 24, 1896, in St. Paul, Minnesota, the son of Edward Fitzgerald and Mollie McQuillan. His father owned a furniture manufacturing business, but after it failed, he found work at Procter & Gamble and the family moved to Buffalo, New York. He would spend the majority of his early childhood in Buffalo, and these formative years revealed him to be a boy of unusual intelligence with a keen interest in literature. When his father was fired from Procter & Gamble, the family returned to Minnesota. In 1913, Fitzgerald began attending Princeton University, but two years later he was forced to leave school because of poor grades and health issues. He returned to school in 1916, but continued to

F. Scott Fitzgerald's birthplace in St. Paul, Minnesota.

F. Scott Fitzgerald
(1896–1940)

F. Scott Fitzgerald (1932). *Courtesy of the Library of Congress, Prints & Photographs Division, Carl Van Vechten Collection, LC-USZ62-88500.*

NOVELIST, SHORT STORY WRITER & SCREENWRITER

Born: St. Paul, Minnesota

Died: Hollywood, California

Buried: St. Mary's Cemetery, Rockville, Maryland

struggle academically, and was placed on academic probation. In 1917, he dropped out of school and enlisted in the U.S. Army.

Zelda Fitzgerald, wife of F. Scott Fitzgerald (1928). *Courtesy of the Library of Congress, Prints & Photographs Division, LC-USZ62-115117.*

He was assigned to an army base just outside of Montgomery, Alabama, and during leave would visit a local country club. It was there that he met and became instantly infatuated with a vivacious 18 year old named Zelda Sayre. She was the daughter of an Alabama Supreme Court judge. He called her frequently and, whenever possible, traveled to Montgomery to visit. At the time, Fitzgerald wasn't the only man Zelda was dating and the competition only made him desire her more. In his journal, Fitzgerald noted that he had fallen hopelessly in love. Ultimately, Zelda would have the same feelings; he had appealed to something deep within her that no other man had ever accomplished: a sense of self-importance. Their courtship was briefly interrupted in October 1918 when he was transferred north. He expected to be sent to France, but was instead assigned to Camp Mills, Long Island. While he was there, the war ended and he was eventually transferred back to Montgomery. By December, Zelda and Fitzgerald were inseparable; he would later describe their behavior during this period as "sexual recklessness." In February 1919, Fitzgerald was discharged from the service and traveled to New York City, where he began to write. The following year, he sent Zelda a letter and proposed marriage. Many of her friends and family were apprehensive about the relationship and pointed out Fitzgerald's excessive drinking and conflicting religious beliefs.

In these early years, Fitzgerald often talked about his desire to be a famous novelist and sent Zelda a draft of his first book, *This Side of Paradise*. He was so smitten with Zelda's charms that he redrafted the character of Rosalind Connage to resemble her. He wrote, "All criticism of Rosalind ends in her beauty" and told Zelda that "the heroine does resemble you in more ways than four." By September 1919, he had completed *This Side of Paradise* and the manuscript was accepted for publication. When he heard the news, Fitzgerald wrote to publisher Maxwell Perkins, urging an accelerated release: "I have so many things dependent on its success, including of course a girl." In November, he returned to Montgomery with the good news and officially proposed to Zelda. *This Side of Paradise* was published on March 26, 1920; Zelda arrived in New York City four days later. They were married on the third of April at St. Patrick's Cathedral. Together they would have one child. Their daughter, Frances Scott "Scottie" Fitzgerald, was born in October 1921, in St. Paul, Minnesota. Zelda allegedly remarked that she hoped her daughter would be a "beautiful little fool." In *The Great Gatsby*, Daisy Buchanan says the same about her own daughter.

Zelda and F. Scott Fitzgerald, circa early 1920s.

The Fitzgeralds soon became the darlings of New York City society, as much for their wild partying as for the success of his novel. In the pages of the New York newspapers, they become icons of youthful vigor, success, and overindulgence. After Fitzgerald's second novel, *The Beautiful and the Damned* (1922), and a collection of short stories, *Tales of the Jazz Age* (1922), were published, they rented a home on Long Island. Soon, reckless spending led Fitzgerald to financial distress, and he attempted to recover by writing a play, *The Vegetable* (1923). The play was a minor success, and failed to provide any real economic relief.

All of this changed with his next novel, *The Great Gatsby*. In it, Fitzgerald made a conscious departure from his previous writing. Unlike his prior works, he intended to edit and reshape Gatsby thoroughly, believing that it held the potential to launch him into a higher stratosphere of literary acclaim. He told his editor that the novel was a "consciously artistic achievement" and a "purely creative work, not trashy imaginings as in my stories, but the sustained imagination of a sincere and yet radiant world." In October 1922, they moved to Long Island. Progress on *Gatsby* was slow and, by May 1923, they traveled to the French Riviera, where he finally completed the novel. *The Great Gatsby* was first published on April 10, 1925, and received mostly positive reviews.

On the heels of this success, the Fitzgeralds traveled to Paris, where they quickly became friends with numerous intellectual and literary types, most notably Ernest Hemingway and Gertrude Stein. Scott's friendship with Hemingway was quite contentious, as many of Fitzgerald's relationships would prove to be. At the outset, Hemingway did not get along very well with Zelda, whom he described as being completely insane. He also accused her of sabotaging her husband's writing career by encouraging his heavy drinking. During this same period, Fitzgerald supplemented his income by writing stories for magazines and screenplays for Hollywood studios. This "whoring" as Fitzgerald and Hemingway called these works, was a point of contention in their friendship. Although his passions always lay in writing novels, only his first novel sold

well enough to support the lifestyle that he and Zelda had adopted. Because of this, and mounting bills from Zelda's medical care, Fitzgerald was constantly in financial trouble. In 1932, Zelda was hospitalized for mental health issues, which brought even more financial distress. Her emotional health would remain fragile for the remainder of her life.

At this point, Fitzgerald moved to Towson, Maryland, where he began writing *Tender is the Night*. It was published in April 1934, and was his first novel in nine years. Critics who had waited years for the follow-up to *The Great Gatsby* were discouraged by its structure and felt that the novel had not lived up to expectations. They viewed it as a thinly-veiled autobiography that told the story of Fitzgerald's marital issues, the damaging effects of living a self-indulgent lifestyle, struggles with ego and self-confidence, as well as his continuing issues with alcoholism. Between 1919 and 1934, Fitzgerald had earned a fortune for his literary works, but he and Zelda had managed to squander almost all of it on their extravagant lifestyle. When *Tender Is the Night* failed to excite interest, financial issues became critical; by 1937, Fitzgerald was in serious debt, despite continued earnings from writing short stories and screenplays. By this time, Zelda had been permanently institutionalized and Fitzgerald's own mental and physical decline was made worse by his continued heavy drinking.

Although Fitzgerald allegedly found screenwriting degrading, he was forced to move to Hollywood to write for MGM studios. He also began writing what would be his fifth and final novel, *The Last Tycoon* (which was published posthumously in 1941). While in Hollywood, he lived with his girlfriend, gossip columnist Sheilah Graham. He had suffered with alcoholism since his college days, but it was during the 1920s that his hard partying lifestyle became legendary. This destructive pattern would leave him in poor health by the late 1930s. During this period, he suffered two heart attacks and was ordered by his doctor to avoid strenuous activity and alcohol. On the night of December 20, 1940, Fitzgerald and Graham attended the premiere of *This Thing Called Love* at the Pantages Theater in Hollywood. As the two were leaving the theater, Fitzgerald experienced a dizzy spell; upset, he said to Graham, "They think I am drunk, don't they?" The following day, as Fitzgerald was writing notes in his newly arrived *Princeton Alumni Weekly*, he suffered a massive heart attack and died.

By the time of Fitzgerald's death, he had been largely forgotten as a novelist. His obituary in *The New York Times* mentioned *Gatsby* as evidence of his great potential that was never fully realized. He was originally buried in Rockville Union Cemetery in Rockville, Maryland. His daughter, Scottie Fitzgerald, worked for many years to overturn the Archdiocese of Baltimore's ruling that her father had died a non-practicing Catholic (because of this he was not allowed burial within the Roman Catholic Saint Mary's Cemetery). On March 10, 1948, Zelda Fitzgerald died in a fire at the Highland Mental Hospital in Asheville, North Carolina. In 1975, both Scott and Zelda's remains were finally allowed to be interred within the Fitzgerald family plot at Saint Mary's Catholic Cemetery in Rockville, Maryland.

F. Scott Fitzgerald died in this home in West Hollywood, California, on December 21, 1940.

Grave of Zelda and F. Scott Fitzgerald at St. Mary's Cemetery in Rockville, Maryland.

"Always dream and shoot higher than you know you can do. Don't bother just to be better than your contemporaries or predecessors. Try to be better than yourself."

WILLIAM FAULKNER

William Faulkner (1954). *Courtesy of the Library of Congress, Prints & Photographs Division, Carl Van Vechten Collection, LC-DIG-PPMSCA-10445.*

NOVELIST & SHORT STORY WRITER

Born: New Albany, Mississippi

Died: Byhalia, Mississippi

Buried: St. Peter's Cemetery, Oxford, Mississippi

William Faulkner was the author of numerous novels, some of which portrayed the decline of the upper classes of Southern culture following the American Civil War. In his works, he often used highly symbolic styles and methods, such as the stream of consciousness technique. He was born William Cuthbert Falkner (as his last name was then spelled) on September 25, 1897, in New Albany, Mississippi, the child of Murry Cuthbert Falkner and Maud Butler. His parents came from wealthy southern families that were reduced to poverty after the Civil War. His paternal great-grandfather, Colonel William Falkner, wrote *The White Rose of Memphis*, a popular novel of the 1880s. William's father owned a hardware store and livery stable in Oxford and later became a business manager at the state university. As a young child, William initially excelled in school; however, by the fifth grade, he became more withdrawn and somewhat indifferent about academics. His future literary endeavors would be heavily influenced by the history and culture of the American South. The women in his life, especially his mother and grandmother, would also play a significant role in the development of his creativity.

At the onset of World War I, he attempted to enlist in the U.S. Army, but was rejected because of his height and weight. He then allegedly enlisted in the Canadian Air Force, where he suffered a leg injury in a plane accident and was discharged in 1918. No one has ever produced any clear documentation that Faulkner was ever actually a member of the Canadian military. In 1919, he began attending the University of Mississippi, but was forced to withdraw because of poor grades. However, some of his poems were published in campus journals. After leaving college, he moved to New York City and began to write while working at various jobs. He returned to Mississippi in 1924 and worked briefly as the postmaster at the university office. He published his first collection of poetry, *The Marble Faun*, in 1924. According to one legend, the misspelling of his last name was caused by a careless typesetting error. When the misprint appeared on the title page of *The Marble Faun*, William was asked whether

Rowan Oak, the home of William Faulkner in Oxford, Mississippi.

he wanted a change. He allegedly replied, "Either way suits me." The following year, he published his first novel, *Soldiers' Pay* (1925), which tells the story of a wounded pilot and his journey home after the conclusion of World War I.

Faulkner met his future wife, Estelle Oldham, when they were teenagers, and from their very first meeting, he knew she would someday become his bride. However, Estelle dated numerous other boys, including Cornell Franklin, who proposed marriage before Faulkner. Although Estelle was not very enthusiastic about the marriage, her parents were insistent that she marry Franklin, who came from a wealthy and respectable family. In 1929, this marriage ended in divorce; two months after the documents were finalized, Faulkner and Estelle were married at the College Hill Presbyterian Church in Oxford, Mississippi. She had two children from her previous marriage, and together she and Faulkner would have another two, one of whom would die in infancy. Their marriage would be compounded by difficulties, largely due to his alcohol abuse and affairs with Meta Carpenter and Joan Williams. During this period, Faulkner continued to write, penning numerous short stories for various national magazines. The income that he generated from these and other works allowed him to purchase a home in Oxford that he named "Rowan Oak."

During the Great Depression, Faulkner, like many Americans, suffered financial hardships. In 1932, he asked his literary agent to sell the serialization rights to his newly completed second novel, *Light in August*, but unfortunately, there were no offers. Then, MGM Studios offered him a job as a screenwriter. While Faulkner was not a fan of the movies, he was in dire need of money and accepted the offer. Hollywood would provide Faulkner with a steady paycheck for the next two decades, and during this period he produced screenplays, including *Slave Ship* (1937), *To Have and Have Not* (1944), and *The Big Sleep* (1946). In 1946, he left Hollywood, vowing never to return.

In his lifetime, Faulkner would publish nineteen novels, six collections of poetry, as well as dozens of short stories. This body of work would form the basis of his literary reputation, and eventually led to a Nobel Prize in 1950. This prodigious output, mainly driven by his need for money, includes one of his most celebrated works: *The Sound and the Fury* (1929). Other well-known novels include *As I Lay Dying* (1930), *Light in August* (1932), and *Absalom, Absalom!* (1936). He was awarded two Pulitzer prizes, one for *A Fable* (1955) and one for *The Reivers* (1963).

Grave of William Faulkner and his wife, Estelle, at St. Peter's Cemetery in Oxford, Mississippi.

Faulkner was a very private person and reluctant celebrity, who only rarely granted interviews. The quality and quantity of his literary output was achieved despite a lifelong struggle with heavy drinking; he rarely drank while writing, preferring instead to binge after a project's completion. Literary historians are in general agreement that Faulkner's alcohol abuse was an escape from the pressures of everyday life and unrelated to his creativity. Whatever the source of his addiction, it undoubtedly weakened his health. In 1959, he suffered a serious horseback riding accident and, on July 6, 1962, suffered a fatal heart attack at Wright's Sanatorium in Byhalia, Mississippi. He was buried at St. Peter's Cemetery in Oxford, Mississippi, and when his wife, Estelle, died on May 11, 1972, she was interred beside him.

Thornton Wilder
(1897–1975)

Thornton Wilder, as Mr. Antrobus in *The Skin of Your Teeth* (1948). *Courtesy of the Library of Congress, Prints & Photographs Division, Carl Van Vechten Collection, LC-USZ62-42494.*

PLAYWRIGHT & NOVELIST

Born: Madison, Wisconsin

Died: Hamden, Connecticut

Buried: Mount Carmel Cemetery, Hamden, Connecticut.

"I would love to be the poet laureate of Coney Island."

THORNTON WILDER

Thornton Wilder was one of the most popular playwrights and novelists of the 20th century. He was born Thornton Niven Wilder on April 17, 1897 in Madison, Wisconsin, the son of Amos Parker Wilder and Isabella Niven. In 1906, the family moved to Hong Kong after his father was appointed United States Consul-General. While in China, Thornton and his siblings attended the English China Inland Mission School at Cheefoo. Because of unstable political conditions in 1912, Thornton, along with his mother and other siblings, returned to the United States and settled in San Francisco. While in high school, Wilder became interested in theater and began to exhibit a unique talent for writing.

Photograph of author Thornton Wilder as a child at the Wilder family cottage at Maple Bluff, Wisconsin, four miles from the family home at Madison. Pictured is Thornton Wilder's father, Amos (standing), with his two sisters, 1900. *Courtesy of the Beinecke Rare Book & Manuscript Library, Yale University.*

After graduating from high school in 1915, Wilder briefly attended Oberlin College, then transferred to Yale University. During World War I, he served with the First Coast Artillery in Rhode Island. After the war, he returned to Yale, where he received a bachelor's degree in 1920. Following college, he traveled to Europe and also taught French at the Lawrenceville School in Lawrenceville, New Jersey. In 1926, he published his first novel, *The Cabala*, which was

Grave of Thornton Wilder at Mount Carmel Cemetery in Hamden, Connecticut.

followed by *The Bridge of San Luis Rey* (1927), for which he was awarded a Pulitzer Prize. Following these literary successes, Wilder resigned from the Lawrenceville School and accepted a teaching position at the University of Chicago. During this period, he published a translation of *André Obey's Le Viol de Lucrece* (1931). In 1938, he was awarded another Pulitzer Prize, this time for his drama *Our Town*. Four years later, he won the prize again for his play *The Skin of Our Teeth*. Other notable plays to follow included *The Merchant of Yonkers* (1938), *A Life in the Sun* (1955), and *Plays for Bleecker Street* (1962). During this same period, he continued to write novels, including *The Woman of Andros* (1930), *Heaven's My Destination* (1934), *The Ides of March* (1948), *The Eighth Day* (1967), and *Theophilus North* (1973).

During World War II, Wilder enlisted in the U.S. Army and rose to the rank of lieutenant colonel in the U.S. Army Intelligence Corps. After the war, he served as the Charles Eliot Norton Professor at Harvard University. Though he always considered himself a teacher, Wilder continued to write all his life. In 1963, he was awarded the Presidential Medal of Freedom by President John F. Kennedy. Five years later, he won the National Book Award for his novel *The Eighth Day*. Although Wilder never discussed his sexual orientation publicly or in his writings, his close friend Samuel Steward is generally acknowledged to have been his life companion. He was introduced to Steward by their mutual friend Gertrude Stein. On December 7, 1975, Wilder died from a heart attack at the home of his sister, Isabel, in Hamden, Connecticut, and was buried at Mount Carmel Cemetery.

Ernest Hemingway
(1899–1961)

Ernest Hemingway writing at a campsite in Kenya (1953). *Courtesy of the National Archives and Records Administration, 192655.*

NOVELIST, SHORT STORY WRITER, & JOURNALIST

Born: Oak Park, Illinois

Died: Ketchum, Idaho

Buried: Ketchum Cemetery, Ketchum, Idaho

"For a true writer each book should be a new beginning where he tries again for something that is beyond attainment. He should always try for something that has never been done or that others have tried and failed. Then sometimes, with great luck, he will succeed."

FROM ERNEST HEMINGWAY'S
Nobel Prize acceptance speech, 1954

Ernest Hemingway's literary standing rests firmly upon a small body of writing that is set apart by its style, emotional content, and dramatic intensity of vision. Because of these works and his intense persona, Hemingway is considered by many to be the most influential American writer of the 20th century. He was born Ernest Miller Hemingway on July 21, 1899, in Oak Park, Illinois, the son of Clarence Edmonds Hemingway and Grace Hall. Both of his parents were highly educated; his father was a well-respected doctor and his mother taught music. For a brief period, they lived with Grace's father, but after Ernest Hall's death, they purchased a larger home several blocks away.

Ernest's early childhood was spent largely fighting the feminine influence of his mother, while fending off the emotional weakness of his father. As an adult, he often professed hatred of his mother, but, ironically, often mirrored her energy and passions. Her insistence that he learn to play the cello became a source of conflict, but

Ernest Hemingway was born in this house on July 21, 1899, in Oak Park, Illinois.

Boyhood home of Ernest Hemingway in Oak Park, Illinois.

Ernest Hemingway and Agnes von Kurowsky (center) at the San Siro Race Track, Milan, Italy (1918). *Courtesy of the Ernest Hemingway Collection, John F. Kennedy Presidential Library and Museum, Boston.*

Ernest later admitted that these music lessons were useful to his writing. Ernest later wrote about his father's lack of courage in the short story, "The Doctor and the Doctor's Wife," and his tragic suicide in 1928 left his famous son with severe emotional scars.

The Hemingway family often spent summers in northern Michigan at their cabin on Walloon Lake and these early childhood experiences instilled in Ernest a lifelong passion for nature and adventure. In high school, he was a good student and star athlete, but yearned for excitement. His first real chance to escape Oak Park came when the U.S. entered World War I. He was eager to serve his country and, in 1917, enlisted in the army. After being rejected because of poor eyesight, undaunted he volunteered for the Red Cross medical service where he served as an ambulance driver.

He was deployed to France and arrived in Paris in May 1918. The next month, he was sent to the Italian Front. It was during this same time that he first met John Dos Passos, with whom he had a rocky relationship for decades. On his first day of duty in Milan, he was sent to the scene of a munitions factory explosion where rescuers retrieved the remains of female workers. He would later detail the carnage of the scene in his non-fiction book *Death in the Afternoon* (1932).

On July 8, 1918, he was seriously wounded by mortar fire, but despite the severity of his injuries, was able to carry a wounded Italian soldier to safety. He sustained severe shrapnel wounds to both legs, underwent an immediate operation and spent five days at a field hospital before being transferred to convalescence in a Red Cross hospital in Milan. For this act of heroism, he was awarded the Italian Silver Medal of Bravery. He later remarked: "When you go to war as a boy you have a great illusion of immortality. Other people get killed; not you ...then when you are badly wounded, you lose that illusion and you know it can happen to you."

While recovering at the hospital in Milan, he became infatuated with a pretty Red Cross nurse named Agnes von Kurowsky, who was seven years his senior. By the time of his release in January 1919, and his return to the United States, he and Agnes had decided to get married. Two months later, she wrote to tell him that she was in love with another man and was calling off their engagement. Hemingway was devastated, and was determined never to be abandoned again. Throughout the remainder of his life, he exhibited the destructive pattern of preemptive desertion of his wives before they had a chance to abandon him.

After the war, Hemingway returned to Oak Park and began a period of awkward adjustment. Not yet 20 years old, the war had created in him a maturity that was at odds with living at home without any purpose or employment. During the summer of 1919, he traveled to Michigan's Upper Peninsula and spent a week camping alone in the backcountry. The trip would later become the inspiration for his short story "Big Two-Hearted River." In the early winter of 1920, Hemingway accepted a job as a freelance writer for the *Toronto Star Weekly*,

Ernest Hemingway and his first wife, Hadley Richardson, Chamby, Switzerland (1922). *Courtesy of the Ernest Hemingway Collection, John F. Kennedy Presidential Library and Museum, Boston.*

but returned to Chicago in September to work as an associate editor for the *Cooperative Commonwealth* journal. It was during this period that he met novelist Sherwood Anderson, who was immediately impressed by his journalistic skills.

In December 1920, Hemingway was introduced to 29-year-old St. Louis native Hadley Richardson. She had come to Chicago to visit the sister of Hemingway's roommate and Ernest was immediately smitten with her kind, nurturing character. They would correspond for several months before deciding to get engaged. They were married on September 3, 1921, in Horton Bay, Michigan. Two months later, he was hired as foreign correspondent for the *Toronto Star*. They first wanted to visit Rome, but Sherwood Anderson convinced Hemingway to visit Paris instead, writing letters of introduction for the young couple. On the surface, Hemingway appeared to have everything he had ever dreamed of: the love of a beautiful woman, a comfortable income, and an adventurous life living abroad.

These early years in Paris were the happiest and most artistically productive of Hemingway's entire life. He and Hadley lived in a small apartment in the Latin Quarter. While in Paris, he became good friends with Gertrude Stein, who would become his writing mentor. It was Stein who introduced him to other expatriate artists and writers, whom she referred to as the "Lost Generation." This term would be popularized by Hemingway in his novel *The Sun Also Rises* (1926). Over time, Stein's influence began to decline, and the two eventually became estranged.

During the summer of 1923, Hemingway traveled to Pamplona, Spain, where he became fascinated with the culture, particularly bullfighting. On December 10, 1923, Hadley gave birth to their only child, John (who was nicknamed Bumby). By the time they returned to Paris, Ernest had published his first collection of short stories and poetry entitled *Three Stories and Ten Poems* (1923). In June 1925, he began to write what would become *The Sun Also Rises* (1926). This novel would become a symbol of the "lost generation," and chronicled the lives of a small group of World War I veterans, all of whom suffered physical and emotional injuries from the war. While writing the novel, Hemingway began an affair with family friend Pauline Pfeiffer, who was a journalist for *Vogue* magazine. In the spring of 1926, Hadley became aware of the affair and filed for a divorce, which was finalized in early 1927. Hemingway and Pfeiffer were married on May 10, 1927, and by the end of the year, she was pregnant and wanted to move back to the United States. Hemingway's longtime friend and fellow novelist John Dos Passos recommended that they move to Key West, Florida.

On June 28, 1928, Pauline gave birth to their son Patrick in Kansas City, Missouri. The difficult delivery was later fictionalized in Hemingway's novel, *A Farewell to Arms* (1929). Six months later, Ernest received word that his father had committed suicide. He was devastated by the news, and prophetically remarked, "I'll probably go the same way." After his father's funeral in Chicago, he returned to Key West and began to write *A Farewell to Arms*, which was published in September of 1929. The novel tells the story of a tragic love affair between an American soldier and an English nurse set against the backdrop of World War I.

Ernest Hemingway's home in Key West, Florida.

Hemingway penned some of his most famous works in this office at his home in Key West, Florida.

On November 3, 1930, Hemingway was injured in an auto accident near Billings, Montana. He severely injured the nerves in his writing hand, and took nearly a year to heal. Returning to Key West after nearly two months in a Montana hospital, Pauline's uncle bought them a house situated across the street from an old lighthouse. This landmark made it easy for Ernest to find his way home after spending many hours drinking and carousing. Pauline gave birth to their second son, Gregory, on November 12, 1931, in Kansas City, Missouri.

In 1933, Ernest and Pauline ventured to Africa, where they embarked on a two-month safari. These experiences provided Ernest with material for several short stories, one of which would later become "The Snows of Kilimanjaro." It was first published in *Esquire* magazine in 1936 and later republished in *The Fifth Column and the First Forty-Nine Stories* in 1938. Upon his return to Key West in early 1934, he began writing his second nonfiction work, *Green Hills of Africa* (1935). During this period, he also wrote *To Have and Have Not* (1937), his only novel of the 1930s.

Always searching for adventure, Hemingway began reporting on the Spanish Civil War for the *North American Newspaper Alliance* in 1937. He was joined in Spain by fellow journalist Martha Gellhorn, with whom he was having an affair. He had become acquainted with Gellhorn in Key West the previous year, and like his

Ernest Hemingway and his third wife, Martha Gellhorn, at the Stork Club, New York City (1941). *Courtesy of Sherman Billingsley's Stork Club/Ernest Hemingway Collection, John F. Kennedy Presidential Library and Museum, Boston.*

first wife, Hadley Richardson, Martha was a native of St. Louis. Like Pauline Pfeiffer, Gellhorn had worked for *Vogue* magazine in Paris. While reporting on the war and openly living with Martha in Madrid, Hemingway wrote *The Fifth Column and the First Forty-Nine Stories* (1938), which included his only play. Never lacking in courage, he was present and reported on the bloody Battle of the Ebro, and was among the last journalists to leave the battlefield on November 16, 1938.

After the Spanish Civil War concluded in early 1939, Ernest returned to the United States, but by then his marriage to Pauline was irrevocable damaged. He then moved to Cuba, where he began living with Martha Gellhorn. His divorce from Pauline was finalized in January 1940, and the following May, he and Martha married. During this period, he was inspired to write his most famous novel, *For Whom the Bell Tolls* (1940). This novel is considered by many to be his most ambitious work, and it was written in a less lyrical and more dramatic style. It sold half a million copies within months of its release and was nominated for a Pulitzer Prize, re-establishing Hemingway's literary reputation. After the success of this novel, Hemingway's literary output was non-existent for a decade. This lapse was caused largely in part by his work as a war correspondent during World War II.

In 1942, while reporting for *Collier's* magazine, he was attached to the U.S. Third Army and witnessed some of the bloodiest battles in Europe. It was during this period that he gained the nickname "Papa" from his admirers, both military and literary. He became increasingly resentful of Martha Gellhorn's long absences as she also served as a war journalist. On August 25, 1944, Hemingway was present when Paris was liberated from the Germans, and contrary to urban legend, he was not the first to enter the city, nor did he liberate the Ritz Hotel. In mid-December 1944, a very sick Hemingway insisted on reporting on The Battle of the Bulge. As soon as he arrived at the front, he was

hospitalized, and before he could recover, the majority of the fighting had concluded. He was awarded a Bronze Star for bravery and service during the war.

Upon returning to London, he met and became infatuated with *Time* magazine correspondent Mary Welsh. On their third meeting, he asked her to marry him, although he was still technically married to Martha at the time. In 1945, after four very contentious years of marriage, he and Gellhorn divorced. Hemingway married Mary Welsh on March 14, 1946 in Cuba, five months later, she would miscarry what would have been their only child together.

Throughout the 1940s, Hemingway suffered from severe bouts of depression that were compounded by the deaths of friends and colleagues, such as F. Scott Fitzgerald (1940), Sherwood Anderson (1941), James Joyce (1946), Gertrude Stein (1947), and Max Perkins (1947). He also suffered from numerous other health issues that had been worsened by years of heavy drinking. In January 1946, he began writing a trilogy that he hoped to eventually combine into one novel entitled *The Sea Book*. However, this project stalled, and his inability to continue writing during this period was a direct side effect of his many mental and physical issues.

In 1948, Hemingway traveled to Europe, staying in Venice for several months. While there, Hemingway became obsessed with 19-year-old Adriana Ivancich, and it was their platonic love affair that would inspire him to write *Across the River and into the Trees* (1950). The novel received numerous negative reviews and in response, a furious Hemingway wrote *The Old Man and the Sea* (1952). He wanted to prove to critics that he still had a talent for writing. It was immediately hailed as a masterpiece and won the 1953 Pulitzer Prize. It also helped renew his celebrity status and reinvigorated him both physically and mentally. He later commented that he believed the story was the best he had ever written. In 1954, he was awarded a Noble Prize for literature.

During the last decade of his life, Hemingway's health and literary output steadily declined. A trip to Africa in 1954 ended in a plane crash, which left him with severe burns and internal injuries from which he would never fully recover. Upon his return to the United States, he was admitted to the Mayo Clinic, suffering from high blood pressure and severe depression for which he later received electroshock therapy. Made bitter by these illnesses that impaired his writing, in the early morning hours of July 2, 1961, he committed suicide. He unlocked the basement storeroom where his guns were kept, went upstairs to the front entrance foyer of his Ketchum, Idaho home, put the barrel of a shotgun into his mouth, and pulled the trigger. Despite the deliberate nature of the act, shockingly, his death was initially labeled an accident. In a press interview five years after her husband's death, Mary Welsh Hemingway admitted that her husband had intentionally killed himself. His brief funeral and burial at the Ketchum Cemetery was witnessed by only immediate family and fifty invited guests.

Home of Ernest Hemingway in Ketchum, Idaho, where he committed suicide on July 2, 1961.

During his final years, Ernest's behavior resembled that of his father, who had also committed suicide. The elder Hemingway may have suffered from hemochromatosis, a genetic disease in which the body is unable to metabolize iron and culminates in mental and physical deterioration. Medical records made available in the early 1990s confirmed that Ernest had been diagnosed with hemochromatosis in early 1961. His sister, brother, and granddaughter would also commit suicide.

After their divorce, Hadley Richardson stayed in France. Among her many friends in Paris was Paul Mowrer, foreign correspondent for the *Chicago Daily News*. On July 3, 1933, after a five-year courtship, she and Mowrer were married in London. She died on January 22, 1979, in Lakeland, Florida, and was buried at the Chocorua Cemetery in Tamworth, New Hampshire.

Pauline Pfeiffer spent the rest of her life in Key West, but made frequent visits to California. She died on October 21, 1951, in Los Angeles. Her death was attributed to shock related to her son Gregory's arrest for lewd behavior. Her autopsy report was revised to state that she had died from a tumor on her adrenal gland. It was theorized that the stress of the incident had caused the tumor to secrete excessive amounts of adrenaline and then abruptly stopped. The resulting change in blood pressure allegedly caused the shock that ultimately killed her. She was buried at Hollywood Forever Cemetery in Hollywood, California, in an unmarked grave.

After divorcing Hemingway, Martha Gellhorn had numerous love affairs. In 1954, she married Tom Matthews, a former managing editor of *Time* magazine. They lived in London, which was to be her home for the rest of her life. They would divorce in 1963, and for the remainder of her life she refused to comment on her relationship with Hemingway. On February 15, 1998, after battling cancer for several years, Martha Gellhorn committed suicide by overdosing on drugs. Her body was cremated and the ashes were scattered in the River Thames.

Following her husband's tragic suicide in 1961, Mary Welsh acted as Hemingway's literary executor and was responsible for the posthumous publication of his memoir *A Moveable Feast,* in 1964, as well as other works. She died on November 27, 1986, in Ketchum, Idaho, and is buried beside Ernest at the Ketchum Cemetery.

Grave of Ernest Hemingway at the Ketchum Cemetery, Ketchum, Idaho.

E. B. White
(1899–1985)

E.B. White with his dog, Minnie, from an undated photograph. *Courtesy of White Literary LLC.*

ESSAYIST, NOVELIST, & POET

Born: Mount Vernon, New York

Died: North Brooklin, Maine

Buried: Brooklin Cemetery, Brooklin, Maine

"Writing is an act of faith, not a trick of grammar."

E.B. WHITE

E. B. White was one of the most influential essayists of the 20th century, largely based on his contributions to *The New Yorker* magazine. He also wrote three children's novels and helped revise what is considered the preeminent guide to writing and grammar, *William S. Strunk's The Elements of Style*. He was born Elwyn Brooks White on July 11, 1899, in Mount Vernon, New York, the son of Samuel Tilly White and Jessie Hart. He attended public schools in Mount Vernon and later attended Cornell University, graduating in 1921. Following college, he briefly worked for the United Press International and the American Legion News Service (1921-1922). He then became a reporter for the *Seattle Times* (1922-1923) and the Frank Seaman advertising agency (1923-1925), where he worked as a production assistant and copywriter before returning to New York City.

In 1925, White published the article "Defense of The Bronx River" in *The New Yorker* magazine and, with help from his future wife, Katharine Angell (who was the literary editor for *The New Yorker*), became a contributing editor for the magazine in 1927. He would eventually become the principal contributor to the magazine's "Notes and Comment" column, which conveyed the ups and downs of everyday life in the big city through amusing and intellectual observations.

In 1929, he published a collection of poetry, *The Lady Is Cold*, and that same year married Katharine Angell. She had two children from a previous marriage, and together they would have one more son. In 1936, writing under the pseudonym Lee Stewart, White wrote the essay "Farewell My Lovely!" for *The New Yorker*. The piece was full of comic descriptions of his memory of the Model T Ford automobile and was the first essay to bring him worldwide acclaim. It was published in book form in 1936 as *Farewell to the Model T*. Two years later, he published another collection of poetry, *The Fox of Peapack and Other Poems*, and also began writing a monthly column for *Harper's* magazine called "One Man's Meat."

In 1945, he published his first children's book, *Stuart Little*, which tells the fanciful story of a talking mouse that is born to human parents. The story was clearly intended to help comfort children who thought of themselves as being different. On the heels of

Grave of author E.B. White and his wife, Katharine, at Brooklin Cemetery in Brooklin, Maine.

this success, he wrote *The Wild Flag* (1946) and *Here Is New York* (1949). In 1952, he returned to children's fiction, penning the classic *Charlotte's Web* (1952). The novel tells the story of the bond between a pig and a spider. It examined the importance of friendship, and also delicately handled the subject of death as part of the cycle of life.

In 1918, Cornell University English professor William Strunk Jr. wrote *The Elements of Style* and privately published it for inhouse use at the university. Later, it was revised and titled as *The Elements and Practice of Composition* (1935). In 1957, the book came to the attention of White, who was a former student of Strunk's at Cornell. He had long forgotten the little book that he described as a "forty-three-page summation of the case for cleanliness, accuracy, and brevity in the use of English." White wrote a feature story about Strunk (who had died in 1946) and his commitment to writing style and grammar. Subsequently, Macmillan & Company asked White to revise the outdated text of *The Elements of Style* for a 1959 edition.

In the coming years, honors began to pour in for White. He was awarded the Gold Medal for Essays and Criticism from the National Institute of Arts and Letters (1960), the Presidential Medal of Freedom (1963), the Laura Ingalls Wilder Medal for his children's books (1970), and the National Medal for Literature (1971). He published his third, and final, children's novel, *The Trumpet Swan*, in 1970, which tells the story of Louis, a swan born without a voice who tries to overcome his disability by learning to play a trumpet. In 1973, he won an honorary Pulitzer Prize for his entire body of literary work. On October 1, 1985, White died at his home in North Brooklin, Maine, from complications related to Alzheimer's disease. He was buried beside his wife, Katharine, who had died in 1977, at Brooklin Cemetery.

Margaret Mitchell
(1900–1949)

Margaret Mitchell (1941). *Courtesy of the Library of Congress, Prints & Photographs Division, LC-USZ62-111609*

NOVELIST & SHORT STORY WRITER

Born: Atlanta, Georgia

Died: Atlanta, Georgia

Buried: Oakland Cemetery, Atlanta, Georgia

"Life's under no obligation to give us what we expect."

MARGARET MITCHELL

Margaret Munnerlyn Mitchell was born on November 8, 1900, in Atlanta, Georgia, the daughter of Eugene Muse Mitchell and Mary Isabel "May Belle" Stephens. Her father was a prominent attorney and her mother was an early women's rights advocate, who encouraged her daughter to advance herself though academics and to write at an early age. She attended Atlanta's Washington Seminary, a private girls-only high school, where her instructors also saw talent in her writing and encouraged its development.

After high school, she attended Smith College in Northampton, Massachusetts, but did not excel in any area of academics. Her professors thought she could write very well, but Margaret was insecure about her abilities. On January 25, 1919, Margaret's mother died from complications associated with the outbreak of Spanish Influenza. Knowing her death was imminent, May Belle Mitchell had written her daughter a brief letter and advised her: "Give of yourself with both hands and overflowing heart, but give only the excess after you have lived your own life." Following her freshman year at Smith, Mitchell withdrew from school and returned to Atlanta to help her father. Although she had planned to return to college at some point, she never went back. She would later confide to a friend that giving up college and her dreams to keep house and take her mother's place in society meant giving up all worthwhile things.

Margaret (who preferred to be called Peggy) made her Atlanta society debut during the winter of 1920. She was, in her own words, an "unscrupulous flirt" and over the next few years was engaged to five men, but maintained that she neither lied to, nor consciously misled any of them. On September 2, 1922, she married Berrien "Red" Upshaw, despite her family's disapproval. The couple resided at the Mitchell home with her father, but after only two months, the marriage was over and Upshaw moved out. Apparently, she suffered both physical and emotional abuse, which was a direct result of Upshaw's heavy drinking and controlling nature. He agreed to an uncontested divorce after Mitchell agreed not to press assault charges against him. The divorce was finalized in October 1924. Soon after, she began to date John Marsh, a copy editor for the Associated Press. Nine months later, they were married. While still legally married to her first husband and desperately in need of cash, Mitchell had accepted an assignment writing feature articles for *The Atlanta Journal Sunday Magazine*.

Grave of Margaret Mitchell at Oakland Cemetery in Atlanta, Georgia.

In 1926, Mitchell suffered a serious ankle injury in an automobile accident. Due to poor medical treatment, the injury never healed properly, and she was forced to stay home and end her journalism career. During her two years writing for *The Atlanta Journal,* she had penned over 200 feature articles and stories. After several months of doing nothing, Margaret's husband suggested she write a book to occupy her time, and for the next decade, she worked diligently on a Civil War-era novel that drew upon her own experiences growing up in the South. This novel eventually became *Gone with the Wind,* and was published in 1936. It was an immediate success, and was well received by critics. At the time of its release, it was one of the highest selling novels in American literary history and, in 1937, was awarded the Pulitzer Prize.

During World War II, Mitchell was an active volunteer for the American Red Cross and also helped to raise bonds for the war effort. She was the leading sponsor of the building of two naval vessels both named the USS *Atlanta*. On the evening of August 11, 1949, Mitchell was struck by an automobile as she crossed the intersection of Peachtree and 13th Streets in Atlanta. She died at Grady Hospital five days later, never regaining consciousness. The driver, Hugh Gravitt, claimed that Mitchell had darted in front of his car, and he tried to avoid hitting the author. He was arrested for drunk driving and was eventually convicted of involuntary manslaughter. Gravitt served only ten months in jail. Mitchell was buried at Oakland Cemetery in Atlanta. Following her death, it was discovered that in her teenage years she had written several short stories that included "The Big Four," "Little Sister," and a novella, *Lost Laysen,* which have since been posthumously published.

John Steinbeck
(1902–1968)

John Steinbeck (1966). *Courtesy of the Library of Congress, Prints & Photographs Division, New York World-Telegram & Sun Collection, LC-USZ62-109602.*

NOVELIST

Born: Salinas, California

Died: New York City, New York

Buried: Garden of Memories Memorial Park

Salinas, California

"I hold that a writer who does not passionately believe in the perfectibility of man has no dedication or any membership in literature."

JOHN STEINBECK

John Steinbeck authored numerous novels and his most well-known were about the working classes of American society during the Great Depression. He was born John Ernst Steinbeck Jr. on February 27, 1902, in Salinas, California, the son of John Ernst Steinbeck Sr. and Olive Hamilton. He would live most of his life in Monterey County, California, where a majority of his books were set. After graduating from Salinas High School, he began attending Stanford University, but left school without obtaining a degree. In 1925, he traveled to New York City with hopes of becoming a writer. After four years of limited success, he returned to California and published his first novel *Cup of Gold* (1929), which focused on the Panamanian adventures of seventeenth-century pirate Henry Morgan. That same year, while working at a fish hatchery near Lake Tahoe, he met his first wife, Carol Henning. They were married on January 14, 1930, and had no children together. For most of the 1930s, they would live in a cottage owned by Steinbeck's father in Pacific Grove, California.

He published two more novels in 1933—*The Pastures of Heaven* and *To a God Unknown*—but neither were well-received by readers or critics. Two years later, he published what would be his first commercial sensation, *Tortilla*

Author John Steinbeck was born in this house in Salinas, California, on February 27, 1902.

Flat (1935). The book was an affectionate and humorous story about a group of Mexican-Americans. On the heels of this success, he published *In Dubious Battle* (1936), which was his first attempt at writing about contemporary social issues (that would characterize many of his later and most notable novels). In 1937, he received even greater critical acclaim for *Of Mice and Men*, a tragic story about the complex bond between two migrant laborers. Steinbeck continued these successes with what has been widely considered to be his crowning literary achievement, *The Grapes of Wrath* (1939). Set during the Great Depression, the novel focuses on the migration of a dispossessed family from the Oklahoma Dust Bowl to California and critiques their subsequent exploitation by a ruthless system of agricultural economics. The novel won Steinbeck a Pulitzer Prize and a National Book Award in 1940. It was also adapted into a film directed by John Ford that was named one of the American Film Institute's 100 greatest films of all time.

After the success of *The Grapes of Wrath*, Steinbeck changed course and decided to write about other subjects. He traveled to Mexico with his friend, biologist Edward F. Ricketts, and together they would write *Sea of Cortez* (1941), a nonfiction study of animal life in the Gulf of California. During this same time, his marriage to Carol Henning was beginning to dissolve; they eventually divorced in 1942. That same year, he met Gwendolyn Conger, and they were married on March 29, 1943. Together they would have two sons. During World War II, Steinbeck worked as a war correspondent for the *New York Herald Tribune* and wrote several effective propaganda novels, such as *The Moon Is Down* (1942), which discussed the Nazi occupation of Norway.

After the war, Steinbeck traveled extensively throughout the Soviet Union as a reporter for the *New York Herald Tribune*, which added fuel to the common suspicion of his involvement in Socialism. His novels of this period began to soften in their rhetorical commentary, and while they still contained elements of social criticism, they were much more sentimental in nature. Important works of this period included *Cannery Row* (1945), *The Pearl* (1947), and *The Wayward Bus* (1947). He also wrote several Hollywood screenplays, one of which, *Lifeboat*, was nominated for an Academy Award in 1944.

In May 1948, Edward Ricketts was seriously injured in a car crash and died. Upon returning home from the funeral, Steinbeck was confronted by his wife, who told him she wanted a divorce. He spent the next year in a deep depression over the loss of his marriage and the death of his friend. However, in 1950, he found happiness again when he met and married former stage actress Elaine Scott. The couple moved to New York City, where he published *East of Eden* (1952). The novel was one of his most ambitious works, and he considered it his greatest literary accomplishment stating, "I think everything else I have written has been, in a sense, practice for this."

DID YOU KNOW?

Steinbeck's realistic portrayals of working-class life have often been deemed too realistic by parents and librarians. *The Grapes of Wrath* was banned in several school districts when it first appeared, with censors citing offensive language, references to sex, and anti-establishment tones as the reason for its suppression. His books still draw controversy; *Of Mice and Men* has been one of the American Library Association's Top Ten Most Challenged Books since 1990.

In the later years of his life, Steinbeck's literary output diminished. He traveled throughout the United States in a camper and wrote his last novel, *The Winter of Our Discontent* (1961), and a memoir, *Travels with Charley* (1962). Neither of these works equaled the critical reputation of his earlier writings. In 1962, Steinbeck won the Nobel Prize for literature, and although he was modest about his own talent as a writer, he often spoke openly of his admiration for other writers. At the Nobel press conference, he was asked who his favorite authors were and he replied, "Hemingway's short stories and nearly everything Faulkner wrote." He was awarded the Presidential Medal of Freedom on September 14, 1964. A close friend of President Lyndon Johnson, he helped draft his acceptance speech for the Democratic National Convention. Two years later, he published *America and Americans*, a collection of photographs and essays on American life, which was the last book published during his lifetime. On December 20, 1968, John Steinbeck died from a heart attack in New York City. He had been a lifelong smoker and an autopsy revealed nearly complete narrowing of the main coronary arteries. In accordance with his final wishes, his body was cremated and his ashes were interred at the Garden of Memories Memorial Park in Salinas, California, with those of his parents and maternal grandparents. In 1975, Elaine Steinbeck would co-write a biography of her late husband, *Steinbeck: A Life in Letters*. She died from natural causes on April 27, 2003, in New York City and was buried near her husband.

Gravesite of John Steinbeck at the Garden of Memories Memorial Park in Salinas, California. Steinbeck's flat marker is located to the front/right of the large Hamilton tombstone.

"Think left and think right and think low and think high. Oh, the thinks you can think up if only you try!"

THEODOR SUESS GEISEL

Theodor Geisel, better known as Dr. Seuss, penned over three dozen children's books that often used peculiar characters, odd themes, and quirky rhymes. His books would bring an innovative and colorful twist to the genre of children's literature. He was born Theodor Seuss Geisel on March 2, 1904, in Springfield, Massachusetts, the son of Theodor Robert Geisel and Henrietta Seuss. Prior to Prohibition, his father owned and operated a local brewery. During Prohibition, he worked as administrator of Springfield's parks. As a child, Theodor spent countless hours drawing animals at the local zoo. Although he would later gain fame because of his imaginative drawing style, he never had an art lesson.

After graduating from high school in 1921, Geisel attended Dartmouth College. During his college years, he wrote for several college magazines, including *The Dartmouth Jack-O-Lantern*. His first work in which he used the now-famous pen name "Dr. Seuss" appeared in *The Judge*, where he wrote a weekly column called "Birdsies and Beasties." He then traveled to England and continued his studies at Oxford University in hopes of attaining an advanced degree in English literature. It was during this time that he met his future wife and fellow American, Helen Palmer. In 1927, Geisel withdrew from Oxford without a degree and returned to the United States. On November 29, 1927, he and Helen were married. They would have no children. She was an early supporter of his artistic abilities, and eventually handled all of his business and editorial duties. Helen was an author in her own right, penning several children's books that included *Fish Out of Water* (1961) and *Do You Know What I'm Going to Do Next Saturday?* (1963).

During the late 1920s and 1930s, Geisel wrote articles and drew illustrations for numerous national magazines and was also a successful adverting artist. In 1935, he created a comic strip called *Hejji*, which was serialized nationally in the Hearst syndicate of newspapers. The inspiration for his first children's book came while he was returning home from an ocean voyage to Europe. The rhythm of the ship's engines inspired him

Theodor Geisel "Dr. Seuss"
(1904–1991)

Theodor Seuss Geisel. *Courtesy of the Library of Congress, Prints & Photographs Division, NYWTS Collection, LC-DIG-ds-01037.*

CHILDREN'S FICTION & SHORT STORY WRITER

Born: Springfield, Massachusetts

Died: La Jolla, California

Buried: Ashes scattered

to write a poem, which eventually became *And to Think That I Saw It on Mulberry Street*. The book was rejected by dozens of publishers before it was finally accepted for publication in 1937. Over the next three years, he would publish four more children's books: *The 500 Hats of Bartholomew Cubbins* (1938), *The King's Stilts* (1939), *The Seven Lady Godivas* (1939), and *Horton Hatches the Egg* (1940).

During the early years of World War II, Geisel drew political cartoons for the New York City daily newspaper *PM* and was a vocal supporter of President Franklin Roosevelt and U.S. intervention in the war. In 1943, he enlisted in the army and became the head of the Animation Department, where he produced propaganda and training films. After being discharged from the army in 1945, Geisel returned to writing children's books and moved to La Jolla, California. Notable works of this period include *If I Ran the Zoo* (1950), *Horton Hears a Who* (1955), and *If I Ran the Circus* (1956).

In 1957, he wrote what would become his most famous and endearing book, *The Cat in the Hat*. Legend states that this book was created, in part, because of a bet Geisel made with his publisher who said he could not write a children's book with less than 250 words. *The Cat in the Hat* came in at 236 words. In the book, "The cat in the hat" brings a wacky form of chaos to the home of two bored children on a rainy day. The book has been popular since its publication, and millions of copies have been printed in over twelve different languages. In the coming years, Geisel published numerous children's books that included *How the Grinch Stole Christmas* (1957), *Green Eggs and Ham* (1960), and *One Fish Two Fish Red Fish Blue Fish* (1960). All of these books featured crazy-looking creatures that were based on real animals, and Seuss/Geisel perfected the art of telling great stories with limited vocabulary. He was also an original and unconventional artist, but, at his core, he considered himself to be an educator. His main mission was to teach children that reading was a joy and not a chore.

On October 23, 1967, Helen Geisel died after intentionally overdosing on drugs. She had been suffering from cancer and was in constant pain. She had also been depressed after discovering her husband's affair with family friend Audrey Stone Dimond. Less than a year after Helen's death, Geisel moved to Reno, Nevada, with Audrey, where she established residency to get a quick divorce from her husband. In response to growing public criticism, Geisel commented: "Audrey and I are going to be married about the first week in August. I am acquiring two daughters, aged nine and fourteen. I am rebuilding the house to take care of the influx. I am 64 years old. I am marrying a woman eighteen years younger...I have not flipped my lid. This is not a sudden nutty decision." He and Audrey were married on August 5, 1968, in Reno, by a justice of the peace at the Washoe County Courthouse. No family or friends were present at the brief ceremony. Life with his new wife brought Geisel a sense of creative rejuvenation, and it was she who suggested that he grow a beard for the first time in his life. Never one to interfere directly with her husband's affairs, Audrey viewed her role as a custodian and chief supporter of all her husband's enterprises. On September 24, 1991, Geisel, who had been suffering from jaw cancer, died in his sleep at his home in La Jolla, California. His remains were cremated and scattered at an unknown location.

Before Dr. Seuss, children's books were often boring and predictable; they were intended to instruct, rather than entertain. Though his books sometimes included morals, their main lessons often celebrated the idea of listening to ones' own feelings. Although he never had children of his own, he often stated, "You have 'em; I'll entertain 'em." Of the ten bestselling hardcover children's books of all time, four were written by Geisel.

> *"The poem is a little myth of man's capacity of making life meaningful. And in the end, the poem is not a thing we see, it is, rather, a light by which we may see, and what we see is life."*
>
> ROBERT PENN WARREN

Robert Penn Warren from an undated photograph. *Courtesy of the Library of Congress Manuscripts Division, call number 1228.*

POET, NOVELIST & LITERARY CRITIC

Born: Guthrie, Kentucky

Died: Stratton, Vermont

Buried: Willis Cemetery, Stratton, Vermont

Robert Penn Warren was awarded multiple Pulitzer Prizes in both fiction and poetry. He was one of the key figures that helped kick-start the Southern literary renaissance of the 1920s, 1930s, and 1940s. Later, Southern writers, such as Harper Lee, Eudora Welty, and others, were heavily influenced by his works. He was born on April 24, 1905, in Guthrie, Kentucky, the son of Robert Warren and Anna Penn. He was a very bright child who acquired an early love for classic literature and Southern history.

He began attending Vanderbilt University at age 16, where he met and befriended a group of highly influential young Southern writers who helped found a literary group called "The Fugitives." They published a magazine under the same name. This periodical became highly influential during its brief period of publication and was instrumental in developing what became known as the "New Criticism" mode of literary analysis, which stressed close examination of literature, especially poetry, to uncover how each work functioned as an independent creative object. It also opposed using historical or biographical information to interpret a work. Warren and his group went on to create the "Southern Agrarians," a larger organization that opposed the effects of modernization and certain technologies that they thought were destroying the traditions and values of the South.

Warren graduated from Vanderbilt University in 1925, and then traveled west to attend the University of California, Berkeley, where he met his future wife, Emma Brescia. After attaining a Master's degree in 1927, he traveled to England and attended Oxford University, where, in 1930, he was awarded an advanced degree in British literature. During the summer of 1929, Warren and Emma Brescia eloped. They would have no children, and in 1951, their marriage ended in divorce. The next year, he married Eleanor Clark, and together they would have two children.

Boyhood home of Robert Penn Warren in Guthrie, Kentucky.

In 1930, he began teaching at Southwestern College in Memphis, Tennessee, and four years later, accepted a similar position at Louisiana State University. While at LSU, he helped edit and co-found *The Southern Review*. In 1939, Warren wrote his first novel, *Night Rider*, which was based on the Kentucky tobacco wars of 1905–08. This book would foreshadow much of his later fiction, which used irony, violence, and moral issues to portray historical events. During his time in Louisiana, he observed firsthand the rise of politician Huey P. Long. After Long's assassination in 1936, Warren was inspired to write a novel that was loosely based on Long's life. The novel ultimately became the classic *All the King's Men*, and was published in 1946. This novel was well-received by critics and won a Pulitzer Prize. It was also made into a successful motion picture, that won the Academy Award for Best Picture in 1949.

Warren's other novels include *At Heaven's Gate* (1943), *World Enough and Time* (1950), *Band of Angels* (1956), and *The Cave* (1959). He also published a book of short stories, *The Circus in the Attic* (1948), that is considered by many literary critics to be one of Warren's best works. His poetic works include the long narrative poem *Brother to Dragons* (1953), which dealt with the brutal murder of a slave by two nephews of Thomas Jefferson, and *Promise: Poems, 1954-1956* (1957), which won a National Book Award and a Pulitzer Prize. In 1979, he received a third Pulitzer Prize for *Now and Then: Poems, 1976-1978* (1978). He also penned three historical essays, a study of Herman Melville, a biography of Theodore Dreiser, a study of John Greenleaf Whittier's poetry, and several studies of race relations in America. His last published novel was *A Place to Come To* (1977).

In 1980, he was awarded the Presidential Medal of Freedom by President Jimmy Carter and, six years later, was appointed the first American Poet Laureate. Warren lived the last part of his life in Fairfield, Connecticut, and moved to Stratton, Vermont, where he died on September 15, 1989, from bone cancer. He is buried at the Willis Cemetery in Stratton, Vermont, and a memorial cenotaph was placed at his family's gravesite in Guthrie, Kentucky.

Grave of Robert Penn Warren at Willis Cemetery in Stratton, Vermont.

"Enthusiasm is the most important thing in life."

TENNESSEE WILLIAMS

Birthplace of Tennessee Williams in Columbus, Mississippi.

Tennessee Williams was one of the greatest playwrights of the 20th century, and is best known for his dramas *A Streetcar Named Desire* and *Cat on a Hot Tin Roof.* He was born Thomas Lanier Williams on March 26, 1911, in Columbus, Mississippi, the son of Cornelius Williams and Edwina Dakin. His father was a hard-drinking traveling salesman who spent most of his time away from home. His mother was the typical Southern belle and her emotional state was often unstable. Throughout most of his early childhood, Williams struggled with health issues that left him weak and virtually housebound. Because of his parents' instability, Williams and his siblings often stayed with their maternal grandparents in Mississippi. Many historians theorize that Williams found inspiration in his dysfunctional family for much of his writing.

In 1919, the family moved to St. Louis, Missouri, where Williams' father found work at the headquarters of the International Shoe Company. It was during this time that young Williams first began to use the nickname "Tennessee" (presumably because many of his descendants had hailed from that state). He and his siblings were often bullied by other kids because of their Southern accents; this led him to skip school. He often escaped the pressures of adolescence by reading fiction and writing stories.

In 1929, he began attending the University of Missouri, where he enrolled in journalism classes. During this time, he began to write poems, essays, short stories, and plays, which he submitted to writing contests, hoping to earn extra income. Uninspired with college academics, Williams withdrew from school in 1931 and returned home. He then went to work at the shoe company where his father worked. Two years later, he

Tennessee Williams
(1911–1983)

Tennessee Williams at the 20th anniversary of opening of *The Glass Menagerie* (1965). *Courtesy of the Library of Congress, Prints & Photographs Division, LC-USZ62-128957*

PLAYWRIGHT, NOVELIST, & SHORT STORY WRITER

Born: Columbus, Mississippi

Died: New York City, New York

Buried: Calvary Cemetery, St. Louis, Missouri

Tennessee Williams' home on Duncan Street in Key West, Florida.

enrolled at Washington University, where he only spent one year. He then transferred to the University of Iowa, graduating in 1938 with a bachelor's degree in English. After graduating from college, Williams supported himself by working at various unskilled jobs and struggled to have his literary work accepted. In 1939, with the help of his literary agent, Audrey Wood, Williams was awarded a $1,000 grant from the Rockefeller Foundation in recognition of his play *Battle of Angels*. For the next few years, he continued to write, living off of the grant funds and other sources of income.

In 1943, Williams penned the short story, "Portrait of a Girl in Glass," which he later turned into one of his greatest plays, *The Glass Menagerie*. During the winter of 1944-45, the play opened in New York and Chicago to rave reviews. That same year, it won the New York Drama Critics Circle Award and the Sidney Howard Memorial Award. He followed up the success of *The Glass Menagerie* by writing the play *You Touched Me* (1945), and eleven one-act plays that included *27 Wagons Full of Cotton* (1946). When *A Streetcar Named Desire* opened on Broadway in 1947, New York audiences were well aware that a major playwright had arrived on the scene. *A Streetcar Named Desire* was awarded a Pulitzer Prize for drama in 1948.

While Williams was never fully able to repeat the achievements of *Streetcar,* he continued to write with varying degrees of success. In 1950, he wrote his only novel, *The Roman Spring of Mrs. Stone*, and penned three volumes of short stories that brought him an even wider audience. He continued to write plays, including *Summer and Smoke* (1948), *The Rose Tattoo* (1951), *Camino Real* (1953), *and Cat on a Hot Tin Roof* (1955), which won the New York Drama Critics Circle Award and another Pulitzer Prize for drama. Year after year, he continued to produce quality plays, including *Baby Doll* (1956), *Orpheus Descending* (1957), *Garden District* (1958), *Sweet Bird of Youth* (1959), *Period of Adjustment* (1960), *The Night of the Iguana* (1961), *The Milk Train Doesn't Stop Here Anymore* (1963), *The Seven Descents of Myrtle* (1963), and *In the Bar of a Tokyo Hotel* (1969). Literary critics began to complain that Williams was publicly trying to solve personal problems through many of these plays.

Throughout adulthood, Williams had remained close to his sister, Rose, who had been diagnosed with schizophrenia and was later institutionalized following an ill-advised lobotomy. The devastating effects of Rose's mental illness were strong contributing factors to his later alcohol and drug dependencies. He also struggled with his sexuality from an early age, but by the late 1930s, had fully embraced his homosexuality. In 1945, Williams met and fell in love with Frank Phillip Merlo, who would become his personal secretary. Merlo provided Williams with a period of happiness and stability. Their relationship lasted fourteen years, until infidelities and drug abuse on both sides ended it. Shortly after their breakup, Merlo was diagnosed with inoperable lung cancer and Williams returned to take care of him until his death on September 21, 1963. After Merlo's death, Williams fell into a state of severe depression and began to abuse drugs in an attempt to overcome his sadness and constant insomnia.

Throughout the 1970s and 1980s, Williams continued to write, but was unable to recapture the success of his earlier works. In his 1975 tell-all book *Memoirs,* Williams detailed his struggles with alcohol, drugs, and his sexuality. In 1980, he wrote one of his last plays, *Clothes for a Summer Hotel,* which was based on the love affair between F. Scott Fitzgerald and his wife, Zelda. On February 25, 1983, Williams was found dead in his room at the Hotel Elysee in New York City. His autopsy revealed that he had choked to death on the cap from a bottle of eye drops, further indicating that his use of drugs and alcohol may have contributed to his death by suppressing his gag reflex. Prescription drugs, including barbiturates, were found in the room. Contrary to his expressed wishes to have his ashes scattered at sea, Williams was interred at the Calvary Cemetery in St. Louis, Missouri. He had told friends that he wanted his ashes to be spread at sea near the same spot of those of poet Hart Crane. Williams left his literary rights to the University of the South in Sewanee, Tennessee, and when his sister, Rose, died in 1996, she also bequeathed her portion of her brother's estate to the university.

1– Hotel Elysee in New York City, where playwright Tennessee Williams died on February 25, 1983.

2– Grave of Tennessee Williams at the Calvary Cemetery in St. Louis, Missouri.

Arthur Miller
(1915–2005)

Arthur Miller, circa late 1940s. *Courtesy of the Library of Congress, Prints & Photographs Division, LC-USZ62-105905.*

PLAYWRIGHT, SCREENWRITER & ESSAYIST

Born: Harlem, New York City, New York

Died: Roxbury, Connecticut

Buried: Roxbury Center Cemetery, Roxbury, Connecticut

"I love her too, but our neuroses just don't match."

ARTHUR MILLER
Speaking of his ex-wife, actress Marilyn Monroe

Arthur Asher Miller was born on October 17, 1915, in Harlem, New York, the son of Isidore Miller and Augusta Barnett. His father was an Austrian-Hungarian immigrant who owned a small clothing manufacturing business, and his mother was a school teacher. During the economic downturn of the Great Depression, his father was forced to close his business. Miller was an average student and preferred extracurricular activities, such as sports, to academic endeavors. After graduating from high school in 1932, Miller worked at various jobs to earn enough money to attend college. It was during this time that he began to dream of becoming a famous writer. In 1934, he enrolled at the University of Michigan, where he studied drama.

After graduating with an English degree in 1938, Miller was offered several jobs, one as a screenwriter for 20th Century Fox, and another for the Federal Theater Project, a government agency established to provide jobs in the theater industry. He chose the Federal Theater Project, but Congress closed the project after only one year. Miller then went to work at the Brooklyn Navy Yard; he also wrote scripts for radio dramas. In 1940, he penned his first professional play *The Man Who Had All the Luck*, which opened on Broadway on November 23, 1944, but only ran for four performances. The play's failure nearly derailed Miller's career as a playwright, and still remains one of his lesser-known works. That same year, he met and married his first wife, Mary Slattery, with whom he would have two children. He began writing his next play, *All My Sons*, in 1941, which debuted on Broadway

Boyhood home of Arthur Miller on 3rd Street in Brooklyn, New York (undated). *Courtesy of Susan Abbotson.*

126

six years later. The play was a smashing success and was instrumental in cementing his reputation as a world-class playwright. The play won several awards, including the New York Drama Critics' Circle Award. Miller later wrote about his feelings while watching the audience's reaction to a performance of *All My Sons*:

The success of a play, especially one's first success, is somewhat like pushing against a door which is suddenly opened from the other side. One may fall on one's face or not, but certainly a new room is opened that was always securely shut until then. For myself, the experience was invigorating. It made it possible to dream of daring more and risking more. The audience sat in silence before the unwinding of All My Sons and gasped when they should have, and I tasted that power which is reserved, I imagine, for playwrights, which is to know that by one's invention a mass of strangers has been publicly transfixed.

In 1948, Miller moved to Roxbury, Connecticut, where he built a small studio, and there, in less than a day, wrote Act I of his most famous play, *Death of a Salesman*. Six weeks later, he had completed the rest of the play. It premiered on Broadway on February 10, 1949, and won a Tony Award and Pulitzer Prize for drama. He then wrote *The Crucible* (1953), an account of the Salem witch trials of the 17th century, which contained obvious comparisons to the anti-Communist hearings of the 1950s. The highly controversial nature of this work led to mixed reviews by critics. Not long after its release, the House Un-American Activities Committee (HUAC) began to investigate Miller's activities, and, in 1954, denied him permission to travel to England for the London premiere of the play.

In 1956, Miller's *A View from the Bridge* opened on Broadway in a joint bill with one of his lesser-known plays,

A Memory of Two Mondays. This same year, he divorced his wife and married actress Marilyn Monroe. He met the blonde sex symbol on the movie set of *Bus Stop* and their relationship quickly developed into an affair. In reflecting on his courtship of Monroe, Miller later wrote, "She was a whirling light to me then, all paradox and enticing mystery, street-tough one moment, then lifted by a lyrical and poetic sensitivity that few retain past early adolescence." Miller and Monroe were married on June 29, 1956, in a civil ceremony in White Plains, New York.

Later that same year, Miller applied for a routine renewal of his passport and the HUAC used this opportunity to subpoena him to appear before the Congressional committee. When he appeared before the committee, accompanied by Monroe, Miller gave a detailed account of his political activities. Reneging on a previous promise, the committee chairman demanded he give the names of friends and colleagues who had participated in similar activities. Miller refused to comply, saying, "I could not use the name of another person and bring trouble on him." As a result, he was found guilty of contempt of Congress. In 1958, his conviction was overturned by the U.S. Court of Appeals.

In the months following this ordeal, Miller began to write the screenplay for *The Misfits* (1961), starring his wife. It was meant to be a Valentine's Day gift to Marilyn, but by the time filming began, their marriage was already over. Miller and Monroe divorced on January 24, 1961. He would later say that the filming of this movie was one of the lowest points of his life. The following year, Miller married photographer Ingeborg Morath, and they would have two children.

During the last three decades of Miller's life, he would write numerous plays, including *After the Fall* (1964), *The Price* (1967), The Archbishop's Ceiling (1977), *The American Clock* (1980), *The Ride Down Mt. Morgan* (1991), *The Last Yankee* (1993), and *Broken Glass* (1993). He also wrote a screen adaptation for the 1996 film version of *The Crucible* starring Daniel Day-Lewis. For this, he received an Academy Award nomination for best screenplay. His daughter, Rebecca, married Day-Lewis this same year. In 2002, Ingeborg died from lymphatic cancer and two years later, Miller announced that he was in love with a 34-year-old artist named Agnes Barley. On February 10, 2005, he died from a heart attack after a long battle with cancer at his home in Roxbury, Connecticut. Within hours of her father's death, Rebecca Miller ordered Barley to vacate her father's home. He was buried beside his wife, Ingeborg, at the Roxbury Center Cemetery in Roxbury, Connecticut.

Gravesite of playwright Arthur Miller and his third wife, Ingeborg Morath at the Roxbury Center Cemetery, Roxbury, Connecticut. *Courtesy of Rick Watson.*

J. D. Salinger
(1919–2010)

J.D. Salinger from an undated photograph.

NOVELIST & SHORT STORY WRITER

Born: New York City, New York

Died: Cornish, New Hampshire

Buried: Unknown

"An artist's only concern is to shoot for some kind of perfection, and on his own terms, not anyone else's."

J.D. SALINGER

J.D. Salinger has been characterized as both "the hermit crab and Greta Garbo of American literature." He only rarely emerged from his seclusion, usually to complain that somebody was poking at his shell. Over time, Salinger's refusal of his own fame turned out to be as important as his fiction. He is best known for his only novel, *The Catcher in the Rye*, a portrayal of teenage anguish and loss of innocence. The success of this novel led to public outcry and scrutiny. This only made Salinger more reclusive as he struggled with years of unwanted attention, including a legal battle with a biographer in the 1980s and critical memoirs by his daughter and a former lover.

Boyhood home of J.D. Salinger at 1133 Park Avenue in New York City.

Jerome David Salinger was born on January 1, 1919, in New York City, the son of Sol Salinger and Marie Jillich. At the age of 13, his family moved from the west side of Manhattan to a more upscale location on Park Avenue. He was always a shy child; he had trouble making friends at his new school and his grades began to suffer. During this period, he did show a natural aptitude for acting, although his parents disapproved of the idea.

After graduating from high school, Salinger briefly attended NYU and Columbia University, but soon lost interest in college and began devoting all of his energy to writing. By the early 1940s, he had successfully published several short stories in *The New Yorker* magazine. In April 1942, four months after the bombing of Pearl Harbor, Salinger enlisted in the U.S. Army and was assigned to the Counter Intelligence Corps.

He was eventually sent to England and on D-Day (June 6, 1944) was part of an infantry regiment that landed on the beaches of Normandy. By August, his regiment had fought its way through France to the borders of Germany. In the autumn and winter of 1944, he was an eyewitness to some of the most horrific campaigns of the war, including the Battle of Hürtgen Forest.

Very little information exists as to what Salinger experienced emotionally during those military campaigns, but Salinger's beleaguered biographer, Ian Hamilton, alleged that he suffered from post-traumatic stress disorder and had several mental breakdowns after the war. Salinger, through several protracted legal battles, was successful in suppressing this information from the official biography. After Germany's surrender, Salinger reenlisted and was assigned to Counter Intelligence Corps headquarters in Weissenburg, Germany. It was there that he met and married Sylvia Welter. Salinger and his bride returned to the United States in April 1946, but the marriage fell apart after only eight months and Sylvia returned to Germany. Salinger soon found himself back in New York and living with his parents. He resumed writing for *The New Yorker* and penned some of his most memorable short stories, including "A Perfect Day for Bananafish" (1948), and "For Esmé with Love and Squalor" (1950).

During this period, Salinger began to develop an interest in eastern religions, including Zen Buddhism. Throughout the remainder of his life, he would struggle with different religious belief systems. As the years passed, his writing drew increasingly from these traditions. He then began to write what would become his first and only novel, *The Catcher in the Rye*, which he based on a short story "Slight Rebellion off Madison." The novel was published in 1951, the plot of which revolves around a teenage protagonist named Holden Caulfield and his experiences following his expulsion from a New York City prep school. Salinger later stated that the novel was semi-autobiographical. Initial reviews of the book were mixed, but it spent thirty weeks on *The New York Times* Bestseller list.

In the decades since its publication, *The Catcher in the Rye* has become the unofficial manifesto of a generation of disenchanted youth. Salinger's teenage anti-hero was the original angry young man; his sensitive soul and cynical attitude only made him more irresistible to readers. Other writers, such as James Joyce and Ernest Hemingway had written about angry young men, but Salinger created Holden Caulfield at the very moment that a new, uniquely American teenage culture was being born. After he killed John Lennon in 1980, Mark David Chapman said he had done it to promote the reading of Salinger's book. When John Hinckley Jr., shot President Ronald Reagan a few months later, he left behind a copy of the novel in his hotel room.

Salinger followed the success of *The Catcher in the Rye* with a collection of short stories, *Nine Stories* (1953). He then decided to move to a small cottage in Cornish, New Hampshire, and retire from public life. His new home rested on a large tract of land that insulated him from the outside world, which he found increasingly insignificant and invasive. As the years went by, Salinger's self-imposed exile and reclusiveness only helped fuel public speculation and interest. Although he remained isolated, he continue to write, publishing several volumes of short stories that included *Franny and Zooey* (1961) and *Raise High the Roof Beam, Carpenters* and Seymour: *An Introduction* (1963).

In 1955, Salinger married Claire Douglas, a 19-year-old college student; together they would have two children. Their daughter, Margaret Salinger, wrote in her memoir *Dream Catcher* (2000) that she believed her parents would never have married had it not been for her father's belief in the teachings of Lahiri Mahasaya, which brought the possibility of enlightenment to those following the path of a married person with children. By 1967, Salinger's marriage was breaking up; Douglas would later state that her time with Salinger was lonely and isolating. After divorcing, they continued to live near one another to share the responsibility of raising their two children. Within a few years, Salinger had again enchanted another young woman, who joined him in his self-imposed exile.

In April 1972, *The New York Times* magazine published an article, "An Eighteen-Year-Old Looks Back on Life." The author was a high school student named Joyce Maynard. The article brought Maynard a lot of fan mail, including an admiring letter from Salinger. A long correspondence followed between Salinger and Maynard, who was attending Yale University. Over time, the tone of their letters evolved from fatherly advice to more romantic. At the end of her freshman year of college, Maynard dropped out of school and began living with Salinger. In her autobiography, *At Home in the World* (1998), Maynard portrayed Salinger as a man preoccupied with homeopathic medicine, and who loved old TV shows and movies. She also wrote that she found sexual intercourse too painful to complete and that they never fully consummated their marriage. After only ten months together, and without any explanation, Salinger abruptly asked Maynard to leave.

In 1981, actress Elaine Joyce, the widow of singer Bobby Van, received a fan letter from Salinger. She responded to his note just as Maynard had, and a correspondence followed. As he had with his previous relationship, Salinger arranged a face-to-face meeting. He and Joyce soon became lovers and their relationship lasted until the late 1980s, when Salinger met another woman. Colleen O'Neill was forty years younger than Salinger and was the director of the annual Cornish town fair. They were allegedly married sometime in 1988.

During the last decade of his life, Salinger suffered from numerous health issues and, in May 2009, broke a hip in a fall at his home. He died on January 27, 2010, from natural causes at his home in Cornish, New Hampshire. The location of his final resting place remains unknown. It has been alleged that he wished to have his body cremated and scattered. He once said, "Boy, when you're dead, they really fix you up. I hope to hell when I do die somebody has sense enough to just dump me in the river or something…anything except sticking me in a god damn cemetery…people coming and putting a bunch of flowers on Sunday, and all that crap. Who wants flowers when you're dead? Nobody."

"You don't have to burn books to destroy a culture. Just get people to stop reading them."

RAY BRADBURY

Ray Bradbury was one of the driving forces behind the acceptance of science fiction into mainstream American literature during the 20th century. Through his groundbreaking writings, he was responsible for envisioning countless modern-day technologies. He was born Ray Douglas Bradbury on August 22, 1920, in Waukegan, Illinois, to Leonard Spaulding Bradbury and Esther Moberg. During the late 1920s and early 1930s, Ray's family moved constantly while his parents searched for steady employment. In 1934, they settled permanently in Los Angeles. Bradbury grew up in a loving home, which helped foster a solid foundation for his future creative endeavors. He knew from an early age that he was going to be a writer and, at the age of 12, began writing traditional horror stories that imitated the style of Edgar Allan Poe. After graduating from high school, Bradbury attempted to enlist in the U.S. Army, but was rejected because of bad eyesight. He then turned to writing, and published his first short story "Hollerbochen's Dilemma," in the January 1938 edition of *Imagination* magazine. In the coming years, he would sell stories to numerous science fiction magazines and, by the end of 1942, was writing full-time. In 1947, he published a volume of science fiction-related short stories entitled *Dark Carnival*.

In 1950, Bradbury published another collection of short stories, *The Martian Chronicles*, which reflected upon the many issues that plagued the post-World War II era, such as racism, censorship, and the threat of nuclear war. The book was a critical and financial success, and he followed it by writing another collection of short stories titled *The Illustrated Man* (1951). He published his first novel, *Fahrenheit 451*, in 1953. The novel depicts a bleak depiction of the future of American society where books are outlawed. Bradbury later stated that the novel was not about censorship, but was, instead, a story about how television and the media help to destroy interest in reading and promote a skewed view of learning and limited information. In 1962, he published a second novel, *Something Wicked This Way Comes*, which tells the story of a father's attempt to save his son and a friend from the evil forces of a mysterious traveling carnival.

Ray Bradbury
(1920–2012)

Ray Bradbury (1975). *Photo by Alan Light.*

NOVELIST & SHORT STORY WRITER

Born: Waukegan, Illinois

Died: Los Angeles, California

Buried: Westwood Village Memorial Park

Los Angeles, California

Over his long and varied literary career, Bradbury would write numerous novels, including *The Halloween Tree* (1972), *Death is a Lonely Business* (1985), *Let's All Kill Constance* (2002), and *Farewell Summer* (2006). He also penned dozens of short story collections, plays, screenplays, and children's books. During his lifetime, Bradbury was a staunch supporter of public libraries and actively helped to raise money to prevent their closures. He exhibited skepticism with regard to modern technology by resisting the conversion of his work into e-books stating that, "We have too many cell phones. We've got too many Internets. We have got to get rid of those machines. We have too many machines now." When the publishing rights for *Fahrenheit 451* came up for renewal in December 2011, Bradbury approved his novel for electronic publication, but only if publishers allowed the e-book to be digitally downloaded for free. His book remains the only work in the Simon & Schuster catalog where this is possible.

Bradbury married Marguerite McClure on January 16, 1922, and the couple would have four daughters. At an advanced age, Bradbury retained an excitement for life despite what he described as the "devastation of illnesses and deaths of many good friends." In 1999, he suffered a series of stokes that left him partially disabled and wheelchair bound. Despite this, he continued to write and made regular appearances at science fiction conventions until 2009. He died on June 5, 2012, from an undisclosed illness at his Los Angeles area home and was buried at Westwood Village Memorial Park.

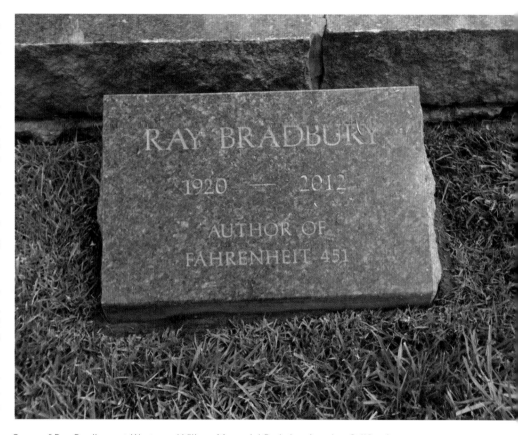

Grave of Ray Bradbury at Westwood Village Memorial Park, Los Angeles, California.

> *"True terror is to wake up one morning and discover that your high school class is running the country."*
>
> KURT VONNEGUT

Kurt Vonnegut's novels are known for their dark humor and social commentary. He was born on November 11, 1922, in Indianapolis, Indiana, the son of Kurt Vonnegut Sr. and Edith Lieber. He began to write in high school and, after graduating in 1940, attended Cornell University. Vonnegut was pressured by his family to study chemistry, but he disliked the subject and received poor grades. He did, however, enjoy writing for the college newspaper. In 1942, he withdrew from college to enlist in the U.S. Army and was sent to the Carnegie Institute of Technology and University of Tennessee, where he studied engineering. His wartime experiences would deeply affect his later writings.

During the Battle of the Bulge on December 19, 1944, Vonnegut was captured and sent to a prisoner of war camp in Dresden, Germany. It was there that he witnessed the horrific firebombing and destruction of the city of Dresden in February 1945. He and a group of fellow American POWs survived the attack in an underground detention center that they'd nicknamed "Slaughterhouse Five." These experiences would later provide the inspiration for his novel *Slaughterhouse-Five* (1969). In the novel, Vonnegut described the horror of the events in great detail, stating, "There were too many corpses to bury. So instead the Germans sent in troops with flamethrowers. All these civilians' remains were burned to ashes." Vonnegut and other POWs were liberated by the Russian Army in May 1945.

Upon returning home, Vonnegut moved to Chicago and enrolled at the University of Chicago. There, he studied anthropology and wrote for a local news bureau. He later admitted that he was a poor student and his Master's thesis was rejected by the university as unprofessional. In 1971, the university accepted his novel *Cat's Cradle* (1963) as his thesis and awarded him a Master's degree. After leaving Chicago, Vonnegut moved to New York, where he found work in the public relations department for General Electric. During this time, he married his childhood friend, Jane Marie Cox, with whom he would have three children. He later wrote about their courtship in several of his short stories. They separated in 1970, but did not divorce until 1979. During this separation period, Vonnegut met, and began to live with, photographer Jill Krementz, who would later become his second wife.

Kurt Vonnegut
(1922–2007)

Kurt Vonnegut from undated photograph.

NOVELIST, SHORT STORY WRITER, & ESSAYIST

Born: Indianapolis, Indiana
Died: New York City, New York
Buried: Unknown

During the 1950s, Vonnegut published dozens of short stories, but often expressed dissatisfaction with them. It is through these stories that readers gained their first taste of his dark sense of humor and biting social commentary. His first novels were often published in paperback and included *Player Piano* (1953) and *The Sirens of Night* (1959). During the 1960s, Vonnegut published additional short stories and four more novels that included *Mother Night* (1961), *Cat's Cradle* (1963), *God Bless You, Mr. Rosewater* (1965), and *Slaughterhouse-Five* (1969), which would bring renewed focus to his earlier works. For the next three decades, Vonnegut continued to write, but after the publication of *Timequake* in 1997, he decided to stop writing novels, though he continued to write for *In These Times* magazine, where he was a senior editor. In 2005, many of these articles were compiled and published as *A Man Without a Country*, which he insisted would be his last book.

Vonnegut often described himself as a cynic, humanist, and nonbeliever. He was a lifetime member of the American Civil Liberties Union and frequently spoke out about moral and political issues. Although he was a nonconformist to the end, Vonnegut held a bleak view of the power of artists and writers to effect change, stating "during the Vietnam War, every respectable artist in this country was against the war. It was like a laser beam. We were all aimed in the same direction. The power of this weapon turns out to be that of a custard pie dropped from a stepladder six feet high." He was a critic of President George W. Bush's administration and the Iraq war. In a 2003 interview, Vonnegut said, "I myself feel that our country, for whose Constitution I fought in a just war, might as well have been invaded by Martians and body snatchers. And those now in charge of the federal government are upper-crust C-students who know no history or geography."

Kurt Vonnegut died on April 11, 2007, after suffering massive head injuries from a fall at his home in New York City. The final disposition of his remains and burial location are unknown.

Home of Kurt Vonnegut in New York City. The author died here on April 11, 2007 after suffering massive head injuries from a fall.

"Great things are not accomplished by those who yield to trends and fads and popular opinion."

JACK KEROUAC

Jack Kerouac (circa early 1960s). *Courtesy of Bettman/Corbis.*

Jack Kerouac
(1922–1969)

Jack Kerouac was one of the principal poets of the Beat Generation and an early leader of the hippie movement, although he opposed some of its more extreme elements. He is best known for his novel *On the Road* (1957), which describes his travels into the American West. He was born Jean-Louis Lebris de Kerouac on March 12, 1922, in Lowell, Massachusetts, the son of Leo Kerouac and Gabrielle Levesque. From an early age, Kerouac dreamed of becoming a writer and, at the age of 11, began writing short stories on various subjects.

He was an outstanding athlete, and was offered several college football scholarships. In 1940, he accepted Columbia University's offer, but, in only his second game of the season, suffered a serious injury to his leg. While recuperating, he began to lose interest in school and often cut classes. After a falling out with Columbia's head football coach, Lou Little, Kerouac decided to withdraw from school and began living with his girlfriend, Edie Parker, at her apartment on New York City's Upper West Side. It was during this time that he met many of the people with whom

Birthplace of Jack Kerouac on Lupine Road in Lowell, Massachusetts.

he would always be associated. The so-called Beat Generation poets included Allen Ginsberg, Neal Cassady, John Clellon Holmes, and others.

In 1942, Kerouac joined the Merchant Marines and, the following year, enlisted in the U.S. Navy. He lasted just over a week at boot camp and the qualities that made him a literary icon are the same ones that rendered him inappropriate for military service: self-determination, imagination, and recklessness. According to his military records, Kerouac

NOVELIST, POET, & SHORT STORY WRITER

Born: Lowell, Massachusetts

Died: St. Petersburg, Florida

Buried: Edson Cemetery, Lowell, Massachusetts

was found to be mentally unfit for service; doctors wrote that "neuropsychiatric examination disclosed auditory hallucinations, ideas of reference and suicide, and a rambling, grandiose, philosophical manner." He was sent to the Naval Hospital in Bethesda, Maryland, and, eventually, was honorably discharged. After leaving the Navy, he began to write what would be his first novel, *The Sea is My Brother*. Kerouac allegedly viewed the work as a disappointment and never actively sought its publication during his lifetime. It was not officially published until 2011, over sixty years after his death.

In 1944, Kerouac was arrested as an accessory after the fact to the murder of David Kammerer (who had been stalking Lucien Carr). According to Carr's version of the event, he and Kammerer were sitting near Riverside Park on the evening of August 13, 1944, when Kammerer made an unwelcome sexual advance. When Carr rejected Kammerer, he was physically attacked. In desperation, Carr stabbed Kammerer with a knife and then dumped the body into the Hudson

The apartment in Ozone Park, Queens, New York, where Jack Kerouac lived with his parents briefly while writing some of his earliest works.

River. He then allegedly went to the apartment of another friend, William Burroughs, who helped dispose of some of Kammerer's belongings. Burroughs then instructed Carr to turn himself in to the police. Carr then sought out Kerouac, who helped him dispose of the murder weapon. Carr then went to his mother's house, and then to the police, where he confessed to the killing. Kerouac was arrested as a material witness, and his father refused to post bail. He then turned to his girlfriend, Edie Parker, whose parents agreed to post bond, if Kerouac agreed to marry their daughter. On August 22, 1944, Kerouac and Parker were married at the jail.

Carr eventually plead guilty to manslaughter and served two years in prison. The incident would inspire Kerouac and Burroughs to collaborate on a novel entitled *And the Hippos Were Boiled in Their Tanks,* which was not published (in its entirety) until 2008. Following his release from jail, Kerouac and Parker moved to Grosse Point, Michigan, but within the year, their marriage was annulled. He then moved back to his parents' home in the Ozone Park neighborhood of Queens, New York. It was during this time that he began to write what would become his first officially published novel, *The Town and the City* (1950), a fictionalized account of Kerouac's life in New York City during the 1940s.

In 1947, Kerouac began what would eventually become a three-year journey throughout the American West that would inspire his second, and greatest, novel *On the Road* (1957). After returning to New York in 1950, he met Joan Haverty. They were married on November 17, 1950, and for a brief period, they lived with Kerouac's parents before renting their own apartment. During this time, Kerouac was writing *On the Road*, which was quasi-autobiographical in nature and describes his road-trip across the United States with Neal Cassady. Although the work was completed quickly, Kerouac had a difficult time finding a publisher. The novel was rejected because of its experimental writing style and its sympathetic tone towards minorities and marginalized social groups of post-war America. Many editors were also uncomfortable with the idea of publishing a book that contained what were, for the era, graphic descriptions of drug use and homosexual behavior. It was finally accepted for publication by Viking Press in 1957.

In June 1951, Haverty became pregnant, but Kerouac insisted she have an abortion. The couple fought often, and she refused the procedure. The couple eventually separated and divorced. On February 6, 1942, Janet Michelle Kerouac was born. He would deny paternity for years, but blood tests eventually proved that she was, indeed, his daughter. Kerouac would not meet his daughter until ten years after her birth.

During the 1950s, Kerouac continued to write and travel, but suffered from severe bouts of depression that were amplified by heavy drinking and drug use. He wrote many novels during this period, including *Visions of Cody* (1952), *Dr. Sax* (1952), *Maggie Cassidy* (1953), *Mexico City Blues* (1955), *Tristessa* (1955), *Visions of Gerard* (1956), *The Scripture of the Golden Eternity* (1956), and *Old Angel Midnight* (1956). He moved to Orlando, Florida, in

Home of Jack Kerouac in Orlando, Florida

July 1957, to await the release of *On the Road*. With its publication, he became instantly famous. Unable to live up to the fictional image he had presented in his novel, Kerouac began to act irrationally and drink heavily. Because of this, his momentum as a serious writer was completely disrupted. In 1961, he briefly traveled to Big Sur, California, where he hoped to rediscover his writing talents, but instead of helping him, the isolation made him even more depressed. He quickly returned to San Francisco and began to drink again. He went on to detail these experiences in his novel *Big Sur* (1962). Defeated and depressed, he moved back to New York and began living with his mother. Although he would continue to write, his works were very disjointed.

Throughout his lifetime, Kerouac failed to sustain any long-term romantic relationships, but in 1966, he married a childhood friend, Stella Sampas. They lived in Lowell, Massachusetts, for a brief period and then moved to St. Petersburg, Florida, where he began to write his last novel, *Vanity of Duluoz* (1968). On October 21, 1969, Jack Kerouac died. The previous night, he had been sitting in his favorite chair when he suddenly began to throw up large amounts of blood and lost consciousness. He was transported to St. Anthony Hospital in St. Petersburg, Florida, and died the following morning, never having regained consciousness. His death at the age of 47 was determined to be caused by cirrhosis of the liver and an untreated hernia, which he had sustained in a bar fight a week prior to his death. He was buried at Edson Cemetery in his hometown of Lowell, Massachusetts. Kerouac's mother, Gabrielle, inherited her son's estate and when she died in 1973, Stella inherited the rights to her husband's literary works, but this was fought by family members and eventually overturned. Kerouac's only child, Janet, died on June 5, 1996, following surgery, and had no children.

Grave of Jack Kerouac at the Edson Cemetery in Lowell, Massachusetts.

Truman Capote
(1924–1984)

Truman Capote (1959). *Courtesy of the Library of Congress, Prints & Photographs Division, NYWT Collection, LC-USZ62-119336.*

NOVELIST & SHORT STORY WRITER

Born: New Orleans, Louisiana

Died: Los Angeles, California

Buried: Westwood Village Memorial Park, Los Angeles & Crooked Pond, Long Island, New York

"Life is a moderately good play with a badly written third act."

TRUMAN CAPOTE

Truman Capote is best known for his nonfiction work *In Cold Blood*, but because of the themes and focus of his early works, critics have tended to categorize him as a Southern Gothic writer. He was born Truman Steckfus Persons on September 30, 1924, in New Orleans, Louisiana, the child of Lillie Mae Faulk and Archulus Persons. Capote's early childhood was marked by periods of instability and poverty. His parents separated and eventually divorced and, at the age of four, he was sent to live with relatives in Monroeville, Alabama. There he befriended Harper Lee, the future author of *To Kill a Mockingbird*. He was a very intelligent child and taught himself to read and write at an early age. The images and early experiences of the rural South would play a profound role in his later writings.

Truman's mother married Joe Capote in 1933; he was a successful businessman and lived in New York City. Truman soon joined them and started using his stepfather's surname. As a teenager, he became uninterested in academics and dropped out of high school after being offered a job as a copy boy at *The New Yorker*. While at the magazine, he attracted the attention of many of the city's literary and social elite because of his flamboyant wardrobe and personality. In 1942, Capote wrote his first short story, "Miriam," which was published in *Mademoiselle* magazine. The story won the O. Henry Award for best first-published story in 1946. Capote published his first novel, *Other Voices, Other Rooms,* in 1948. The book's provocative dust jacket photo of the author caused a frenzy of media interest in the young novelist; because of this, the novel remained on *The New York Times* Bestseller List for nine weeks.

In 1949, he followed these successes by writing a volume of short stories, *A Tree of Night and Other Stories*. Now a celebrated author, Capote quickly embraced the extravagant lifestyle of New York's high society and party atmosphere. In the early 1950s, he began writing scripts and screenplays for Broadway and Hollywood. In 1956, he wrote a series of articles for *The New Yorker*, which eventually became his first nonfiction work, *The Muses Are Heard* (1956). Two years later, he published *Breakfast at Tiffany's: A Short Novel and Three Stories* (1958). The novel's style prompted playwright Norman Mailer to call Capote "the most perfect writer of my generation."

Truman Capote's home in Brooklyn Heights, New York.

Riding the wave of success of these and other works, Capote began an investigation into what would eventually become his most famous nonfiction work, *In Cold Blood*. The book was inspired by the brutal 1959 murder of the Clutter family in rural Holcomb, Kansas. Fascinated by the story, Capote traveled with fellow author Harper Lee to Holcomb and began to explore the crime. Over the course of the next few years, he became acquainted with everyone involved in the investigation. During the first few months of the investigation, Harper Lee was instrumental in befriending the wives of those Capote wanted to interview for his book. It was finally completed and published serially in *The New Yorker* and then in book form in 1966. The book brought Capote great praise from the literary community and was instrumental in pioneering a new genre of literature: the nonfiction novel. After completing *In Cold Blood*, Capote continued to write, but never penned another novel.

During the height of his celebrity, Capote had many friends, including actors, authors, critics, royalty, and aristocrats, whom he entertained in lavish style. In 1966, in honor of *Washington Post* publisher Katharine Graham, Capote hosted the now famous "Black & White Ball," a themed costume party widely regarded as one of the most important social events of the 1960s. In his personal life, Capote openly acknowledged his homosexuality and, for most of his adulthood, had an intimate, non-exclusive relationship with author Jack Dunphy. They remained intimate companions from their first meeting in 1948 until Capote's death. On August 25, 1984, Capote died at the Los Angeles area home of Joanne Carson, ex-wife of Johnny Carson. According to the autopsy report, he died from liver disease complicated by phlebitis and multiple drug intoxication. His remains were cremated, and his ashes were interred at Westwood Village Memorial Park in Los Angeles. When Jack Dunphy died in 1992, a small portion of Capote's ashes were mingled and scattered with Dunphy's at Crooked Pond on Long Island, New York.

Portions of Truman Capote's remains are interred within this crypt at Westwood Village Memorial Park, Los Angeles, California.

Flannery O'Connor
(1925–1964)

Flannery O'Connor. *Photo by Joe McTyre via Library of Congress.*

NOVELIST & SHORT STORY WRITER

Born: Savannah, Georgia

Died: Milledgeville, Georgia

Buried: Memory Hill Cemetery, Milledgeville, Georgia

"It is better to be young in your failures than old in your successes."

FLANNERY O'CONNOR

Mary Flannery O'Connor was born on March 25, 1925, in Savannah, Georgia, the only child of Edwin O'Connor and Regina Cline. In early childhood, she developed an interest in writing. In 1937, her father was diagnosed with lupus, an autoimmune disease that eventually led to his death in 1941. This tragedy had a devastating effect on 15-year-old Mary. After graduating from high school in 1942, O'Connor began attending the Georgia State College for Women, where she volunteered as an editor for the college's magazine. She graduated with a degree in social sciences in 1945, and the following year was accepted into the celebrated Iowa Writers' Workshop at the University of Iowa, where she began to study journalism. While in Iowa, she became friends with numerous writers, critics, and editors that included Robert Penn Warren and Andrew Lytle. It was Lytle who helped her publish several short stories in the *Sewanee Review*, for which he was editor.

O'Connor was diagnosed with lupus in 1951 and returned to live with her mother near Milledgeville, Georgia. Although she was only expected to live five more years, she miraculously lived for fourteen. Despite her illness, O'Connor was extremely disciplined, and devoted each morning to her writings. She possessed a keen ear for Southern dialects and a fine sense of irony and comic timing; with the combination of these skills, she would produce some of the greatest works in American literature. She was a devout Catholic living in the Protestant-dominated South and often lectured on faith and literature. She never married, relying on letter writing, and a close relationship with her mother for companionship.

Her two novels, *Wise Blood* (1952) and *The Violent Bear It Away* (1960), both had similar themes that revolved around religion. She often referred to her works as stories about original sin; many readers found the overuse of violence unnecessary, but O'Connor believed that it was essential to the storyline. In discussing her writing style, she wrote, "Anything that comes out of the South is going to be called grotesque by the northern reader, unless it is grotesque, in which case it is going to be called realistic." She would also pen several volumes of short stories that included *A Good Man Is Hard to Find and Other Stories* (1955) and *Everything That Rises Must Converge* (1965).

Flannery O'Connor lived the last years of her life at her mother's "Andalusia," estate, near Milledgeville, Georgia.

In early 1964, O'Connor had surgery to remove a fibroid tumor that unfortunately reactivated her lupus, which had been in remission. She died on August 3, 1964, at the Baldwin County Hospital in Milledgeville, Georgia, and was buried at Memory Hill Cemetery. In 1972, O'Connor's *The Complete Stories* was published, for which she was posthumously awarded the National Book Award. The honor was usually given to a living writer, but judges deemed this work so deserving that an exception was made to honor O'Connor's lifetime achievements. In 1979, *The Habit of Being*, a collection of her correspondence, was published. These letters revealed a great deal about O'Connor's life, writing habits, and religious convictions. It, too, was awarded numerous honors and was named one of the twelve most influential religious books of the decade by *Christian Century* magazine.

Sylvia Plath
(1932–1963)

Sylvia Plath (undated photograph). *Courtesy of Bettman/Corbis.*

NOVELIST, POET & SHORT STORY WRITER

Born: Boston, Massachusetts

Died: London, England

Buried: St. Thomas the Apostle Churchyard

Heptonstall, Yorkshire, England

"Perhaps when we find ourselves wanting everything, it is because we are dangerously close to wanting nothing."

SYLVIA PLATH

Controversy continues to surround the life, writings, and tragic death of poet Sylvia Plath. Today, most literary historians agree that her works helped spearhead the genre of confessional poetry that began to emerge in the 1950s and 1960s. She was born on October 27, 1932, in Boston, Massachusetts, the daughter of Otto Plath and Aurelia Schober. Her father was a well-known professor of biology at Boston University and his death in 1940 would have a profound effect on Sylvia. As a child, she was a good student and teachers praised her writing abilities. At the age of 8, her first poem was published in the *Boston Herald*.

Plath's first short story, "And Summer Will Not Come Again," was published in *Seventeen* magazine in August 1950, and that fall, she began attending Smith College in Northhampton, Massachusetts. At college, she continued to excel academically and socially. In 1952, she entered a writing contest and won a summer internship as a guest editor spot at *Mademoiselle* magazine. Her time in New York City was not what she had hoped for, and this disappointment began a downward spiral of depression. Many of the events that took place during her time in New York were later used as inspiration for her only novel, *The Bell Jar* (1963). In August 1953, severely depressed, Plath attempted what would be the first of many suicide attempts. She was hospitalized for six months and returned to college in February 1953. She graduated the following June, and was awarded a Fulbright scholarship to Cambridge University, where she continued actively writing poetry and met her future husband, poet Ted Hughes.

She met Hughes on February 26, 1956, at a party celebrating the publication of his newest collection of poetry. She had come to the party with the specific intention of meeting Hughes and another poet, Lucas Myers. Although there was a strong physical attraction between Plath and Hughes, they did not meet again for another month. After a whirlwind romance of only three months, they were married on June 16, 1956, at St. George the Martyr Holborn Church in Camden, England. They would have two children. Hughes' biographers note that at the time of their marriage, Plath had not told Hughes about her history of depression and suicide attempts. These details were uncovered much

Sylvia Plath and Ted Hughes' apartment at Chalcot Square, London. It was here that Hughes met Assia Wevill, with whom he would have an affair, later causing an end of their marriage.

later in the marriage, but Hughes has commented that although they had their difficulties, they both felt happy and supported each other's writing careers.

In early 1957, after earning a graduate degree from Cambridge, Plath and Hughes moved to the United States, where she accepted a teaching position at Smith College. After a year, she quit, finding it difficult to both teach and write. They then moved to Boston, where she found a job as a receptionist for the psychiatric unit of Massachusetts General Hospital. In the evenings, she took creative writing classes taught by poet Robert Lowell. It was during this time that she also befriended poet Anne Sexton. Both Sexton and Lowell would have a profound influence on Plath's development as a writer. In 1959, she and Hughes moved back to England, where she continued to write and published her first book of poetry, *The Colossus* (1960), which was well-received by critics.

In the coming years, Plath's writing career flourished, but she could not escape the tragedy that would soon take over her personal life. In 1961, before moving to a country home in Devon, England, she and Hughes subleased their London flat to Assia and David Wevill. Hughes was immediately attracted to Assia, and they soon began an affair. In July 1962, Plath uncovered the affair and moved out. Later that fall, she experienced a great burst of creativity and began writing many of the personal poems upon which her literary reputation now stands. During this brief period, she would write twenty-six of the poems of her posthumously published *Ariel* (1965). Considered to be her finest work, critics were shocked by its violent and vivid descriptions of suicide and death. In December 1962, she returned to London with her children and rented a flat at 23 Fitzroy Road, only a few blocks from the home she had shared with Hughes. Poet William Butler Yeats had once lived in the house, and Plath was pleased by this fact and considered it a good omen.

The winter of 1962-63 was one of the coldest in over a century. The pipes froze, her children were constantly sick, and the house had no telephone. Because of this, and other factors, Plath's depression returned, but she continued to write and penned her only novel, *The Bell Jar* (which was posthumously published in 1963). The novel is semi-autobiographical in nature and details the main character's descent into mental illness, which paralleled Plath's own experiences with depression.

Sylvia Plath's apartment on Fitzroy Road in Primrose Hill, London. It was here on February 11, 1963, that Plath committed suicide. The apartment was also the home of famed poet and playwright, William Butler Yeats.

Grave of Sylvia Plath at St. Thomas a Beckett and St. Thomas the Apostle Churchyard in Heptonstall, Yorkshire, England.

On the morning of February 11, 1963, Plath was found dead in her apartment. Tragically, she had committed suicide by intentionally inhaling lethal gas from her kitchen's oven. She was buried at St. Thomas the Apostle Churchyard in Heptonstall, Yorkshire, where her tombstone is inscribed: "Even amidst fierce flames the golden lotus can be planted." Over the years, Plath's grave marker has been vandalized by fans who have attempted to remove "Hughes" from the stone. The damage has been repaired numerous times, and during the repair process, the grave was left unmarked. Ironically, this has only infuriated mourners, who have publicly accused Ted Hughes of dishonoring Plath's legacy by leaving her grave unmarked for brief periods of time.

John Updike was a master of many genres. He wrote in an intellectual and powerful style that included clever insight into the sadness, frustrations, and triviality of American life. He won virtually every literary award, including two Pulitzer Prizes and two National Book Awards, and was the youngest person ever elected to the National Institute of Arts and Letters.

John Hoyer Updike was born on March 18, 1932, in Reading, Pennsylvania, the only child of Wesley Russell Updike and Linda Grace Hoyer. It was his mother who encouraged him to write and draw. In his childhood, Updike was a fan of witty books and mysteries, which he devoured in mass quantities. As a young boy, he aspired to become a cartoonist and was an excellent student, becoming co-valedictorian of his high school. He received a scholarship to attend Harvard University, where he majored in English and wrote and drew for *The Harvard Lampoon*.

Before graduating *summa cum laude* from Harvard in 1954, Updike met and married Mary Pennington, a student at Radcliffe. That same year, he sold a short story and a poem to *The New Yorker* and moved to England to study at Oxford's Ruskin School of Drawing and Fine Art. During this time, Mary gave birth to their first child. After returning to the United States, Updike and his family moved to New York City, where he became a regular contributor to *The New Yorker*. In 1957, after the birth of their second child, the family moved to Boston's North Shore area, where he stayed for the remainder of his life. Updike maintained ties with *The New Yorker*, and began to write full-time, penning his first book of poetry, *The Carpentered Hen and Other Tame Creatures*, in 1958.

The following year, he wrote his first novel, *The Poorhouse Fair* (1959), which was followed by *Rabbit, Run* (1960) and *The Centaur* (1963). *Rabbit, Run* featured his most enduring character, named Harry "Rabbit" Angstrom, a former high school basketball star and middle-class idealist. His 1968 novel *Couples* inspired a *Time* magazine cover story on his life. In the 1970s, Updike created a new character, protagonist Henry Bech, who was featured in *Bech: A Book* (1970), and followed this with a reappearance of Harry Angstrom in *Rabbit Redux* (1971). In 1974, Updike, a longtime

John Updike
(1932–2009)

John Updike (circa 2000). *Courtesy of Francine Fleischer/Corbis.*

NOVELIST, POET, & SHORT STORY WRITER

Born: Reading, Pennsylvania

Died: Danvers, Massachusetts

Buried: Manchester, Massachusetts and the Robeson Lutheran Church Cemetery, Plowville, Pennsylvania

Grave of John Updike at the Robeson Lutheran Churchyard, Plowville, Pennsylvania. *Courtesy of Michael Updike.*

activist for causes involving the Soviet Union, joined Arthur Miller and others in demanding that the Soviet government stop persecuting Alexander Solzhenitsyn, the author of *One Day in the Life of Ivan Denisovich*. In 1976, he divorced his wife, Mary, and the following year married Martha Ruggles Bernhard.

In the coming years, he wrote numerous novels and other works that included *Rabbit is Rich* (1981), for which he won the Pulitzer Prize, *Bech is Back* (1982), *The Witches of Eastwick* (1984), *Rabbit at Rest* (1991), for which he received a second Pulitzer, *Gertrude and Claudius* (2000), and *Terrorist* (2006). During his lifetime, he was the recipient of numerous awards that included the National Medal of Art (1989), *America* magazine's Campion Award (1997), and the National Medal for the Humanities (2003). His last book, *The Widows of Eastwick*, was published in 2008, which was a sequel to the novel *The Witches of Eastwick* (1984). On January 27, 2009, Updike died from lung cancer at a hospice in Beverly Farms, Massachusetts. A portion of his cremated remains were placed within a cremation garden of a church in Manchester, Massachusetts. His children were all given a handful of his ashes, which were then buried at the Robeson Lutheran Church Cemetery in Plowville, Pennsylvania. His grave marker was designed in the old, New England style by his son, Michael, and depicts him as a happy soul ascending to heaven.

Back of John Updike's grave marker, which features one of his earliest poems. *Courtesy of Michael Updike.*

iterature of the 20th century, and especially that of contemporary America, is best defined by the rules it broke, rather than any styles it created. It was during this period that American literature finally came into its own in the academic world. The works of Melville, Twain, and other major American authors were finally taught in universities as subjects of academic study. This newfound interest in American writers and the literature they created helped propel America's literary reputation around the world.

In the aftermath of World War II, American writers found themselves with new problems: the pre-war world had been obliterated, and a whole new world had been created. Postwar writers began to concern themselves with how to find ways to deal with a world in which the only constant was change. As life changed rapidly, American literature changed. Literature is a reflection of modern civilization, a society that is ever-changing and full of contradictions. There are a few general tendencies that stand out. First, literature often mirrors our collective disillusionment and many modern writers believe that originality is no longer possible. There are only so many combinations of ideas, all that's left is to copy, in as fresh a way as possible, what the previous generations have left behind.

Second, there is a new skepticism about the role of literature itself. Previous generations had created new styles of literature to be subversive; that is, to reject and challenge established standards and customs. In other words, literature set itself apart from society, seeing the masses as people who needed to be enlightened, but who were so bound by social and religious convention and indifference that they probably couldn't be. Many contemporary writers still feel this way, but increasingly, the lines between what is considered to be high and low culture are blurred.

In a third trend, contemporary American literature accepts that everything we know is reliant on our viewpoint. Thus, since there is no truly objective viewer, there is no such thing as truth. There is only my truth and your truth, and those viewpoints can change with the addition of more information. Contemporary American literature takes this idea a step further by calling into question this information, and argues that facts are untrustworthy, influenced by culture, historical perspective, and other undiscovered details. Contemporary literature argues that two contradictory truths can exist side by side. Because of this ability to include contradictions, contemporary American literature, like modern society, sometimes seems at odds with itself. Even as it questions the value of language, it uses language carefully and precisely to demonstrate thoughts. Even as it documents division, it draws fragments into an organized whole, it celebrates diversity and laments alienation, it accepts human character and emotion.

The writers included in this book most certainly penned some of the finest literature of all time and had an enormous impact on the world. To better understand their works, one must first explore the historical context in which these authors wrote and the lives they lived. My intention was to chronicle the lives, works, and burial places of those commonly recognized to be the fifty most significant writers in American literary history. Assembled within these preceding pages were an assortment of concise biographies, some splendid, a few wretched, all striking in their variety and their fates. As we examine the lives and works of these great men and women, it must be noted that ambition, great imagination, and the rejection of literary conventions made their lives and works groundbreaking. It is hoped that knowing more about the personal lives of these great American writers will inspire the reader to re-examine some of their classic works with an eye towards how their lives were often intertwined with their writing.

Alexander, Paul. *Rough Magic: A Biography of Sylvia Plath*. New York: Da Capo Press, 1991.

Alexander, Paul. *Salinger: A Biography*. Los Angeles: Renaissance, 1999.

Allen, Gay Wilson. *Waldo Emerson*. New York: Viking Press, 1981.

Alphonso, C. *O. Henry Biography*. Charleston: Nabu Press, 2010.

Amburn, Ellis. *Subterranean Kerouac: The Hidden Life of Jack Kerouac*. New York: St. Martin's Press, 1999.

American Library Association. "Most frequently challenged authors of the 21st Century." http://www.ala.org/advocacy/banned/frequentlychallenged/challengedauthors. Accessed October 5, 2012.

Arvin, Newton. *Longfellow: His Life and Work*. Boston: Little, Brown and Company, 1963.

Arvin, Newton. *Herman Melville*. New York: Grove Press, 2002.

Associated Press. "Man Reveals Legend of Mystery Visitor to Edgar Allan Poe's Grave." http://www.foxnews.com/story/0,2933,293413,00.html, August 15, 2007.

Baker, Carlos. *Ernest Hemingway: A Life Story*. New York: Charles Scribner's Sons, 1969.

Becker, Jillian. *Giving Up: The Last Days of Sylvia Plath*. New York: St. Martin's Press, 2003.

Benfey, Christopher. *The Double Life of Stephen Crane*. New York: Knopf, 1992.

Benson, Jackson J. *John Steinbeck, Writer: A Biography*. New York: Penguin, 1990.

Benstock, Shari. *No Gifts from Chance: A Biography of Edith Wharton*. New York: Scribner's, 1994.

Berryman, John. *Stephen Crane*. New York: Meridian, 1962.

Bloom, Harold. *Emily Dickinson*. Broomall: Chelsea House Publishers, 1999.

Bloom, Harold. *Stephen Crane*. New York: Chelsea House Publishers, 2002.

Blotner, Joseph. *Faulkner: A Biography*. New York: Random House, 1984.

Blotner, Joseph. *Robert Penn Warren: A Biography*. New York: Random House, 1997

Bosco, Ronald A. and Joel Myerson. *Emerson in His Own Time*. Iowa City: University of Iowa Press, 2003.

Bowers, Claude G. *The Spanish Adventures of Washington Irving*. Riverside Press, 1940.

Bruccoli, Matthew Joseph. *Some Sort of Epic Grandeur: The Life of F. Scott Fitzgerald* (2nd rev. ed.). Columbia, SC: University of South Carolina Press, 2002.

Buell, Lawrence. *Emerson*. Cambridge: The Belknap Press of Harvard University Press, 2003.

Burstein, Andrew. *The Original Knickerbocker: The Life of Washington Irving*. New York: Basic Books, 2007.

Calhoun, Charles C. *Longfellow: A Rediscovered Life*. Boston: Beacon Press, 2004.

Callow, Philip. *From Noon to Starry Night: A Life of Walt Whitman*. Chicago: Ivan R. Dee, 1992.

Charters, Ann and Allen Ginsberg. *Kerouac: A Biography*. New York: St. Martin's Press, 1994.

Cheever, Susan. *Louisa May Alcott: A Personal Biography*. New York: Simon and Schuster, 2011.

Clark, Tom. *Jack Kerouac*. New York: Harcourt, 1984.

Clarke, Gerald. *Capote: A Biography*. New York: Simon and Schuster, 1988.

Clymer, William Branford Shubrick. *James Fenimore Cooper*. Boston: Small, Maynard & Company, 1900.

Conn, Peter J. *Pearl S. Buck: A Cultural Biography*. New York: Cambridge University Press, 1996.

Deldanco, Andrew. *Melville: His World and Work*. New York: Knopf, 2005.

Donaldson, Scott. *Fool for Love: F. Scott Fitzgerald*. New York: Congdon and Weed, 1983.

Edel, James. Henry James: The Complete Biography. New York: Avon, 1978.

Edwards, Anne. *Road to Tara: The Life of Margaret Mitchell*. New Haven: Ticknor and Fields, 1983.

Elledge, Scott, *E.B. White: A Biography*. New York: Norton, 1984.

Faulkner, William. "William Faulkner on the Web: Anecdotes & Trivia." http://www.mcsr.olemiss.edu/~egjbp/faulkner/trivia.html#wl3. Accessed October 5, 2012.

Floyd, Virginia. *Eugene O'Neill: A New Assessment*. New York: Ungar Publishing, 1985.

Franklin, Wayne. *James Fenimore Cooper: The Early Years*, Volume 1. New Haven: Yale University Press, 2007.

Glenday, Michael K. *F. Scott Fitzgerald*. New York: Palgrave Macmillan, 2012.

Gooch, Brad. *Flannery: A Life of Flannery O'Connor*. New York: Back Bay Books, 2010.

Gottfried, Martin. *Arthur Miller: His Life and Work*. Cambridge: Da Capo Press, 2003.

Gross, Robert F., ed. *Tennessee Williams: A Casebook*. New York: Routledge, 2002.

Gruber, Frank. *Zane Grey: A Biography*. Mattituck: Amereon Ltd., 1969.

Gura, Philip F. *American Transcendentalism: A History*. New York: Hill and Wang, 2007.

Haley, James L. *Wolf: The Lives of Jack London*. Basic Books, 2010.

Hamilton, Ian. *In Search of J.D. Salinger*. New York: Random House, 1988.

Harding, Walter. *The Days of Henry Thoreau: A Biography*. Mineola: Dover Publications, 2011.

Hardwick, Elizabeth. *Herman Melville*. New York: Viking, 2000.

Harris, Theodore F. *Pearl S. Buck: A Biography*. New York: John Day Publishing, 1969.

Harrison, Gilbert A. *The Enthusiast: A Life of Thornton Wilder*. New York: Fromm International Publishing, 1986.

Hayman, Ronald. *The Death and Life of Sylvia Plath*. Secaucus: Carol Publishing, 1991.

Hedrick, Joan. *Harriet Beecher Stowe: A Life*. New York: Oxford University Press, 1994.

Hellman, George S. *Washington Irving, Esquire*. New York: Alfred A. Knopf, 1925.

Hobhouse, Janet. *Everybody Who Was Anybody: A Biography of Gertrude Stein*. New York: G. P. Putnam, 1975.

Howarth, William. *The Book of Concord: Thoreau's Life as a Writer*. New York: Viking Press, 1982.

Hoyt, Edwin Palmer. *The Improper Bostonian: Dr. Oliver Wendell Holmes*. New York: Morrow, 1979.

Jackson, Carlton. *Zane Grey*. New York: Twayne Publishing, 1973.

Jones, Brian Jay. *Washington Irving: An American Original*. New York: Arcade, 2008.

Kaplan, Fred. *The Singular Mark Twain: A Biography*. New York: Doubleday, 2003.

Kaplan, Justin. *Mr. Clemens and Mark Twain: A Biography*. New York: Simon and Schuster, 1966.

Kaplan, Justin. *Walt Whitman: A Life*. New York: Simon and Schuster, 1979.

Kazin, Alfred Kazin. "A Genius of Dark Necessity." *New York Times*, September 21, 1980, http://www.select.nytimes.com/mem/archive/pdf? Accessed October 4, 2012.

Kershaw, Alex. *Jack London*. New York: St. Martin's Press, 1999.

Kert, Bernice. *The Hemingway Women*. New York: Norton, 1983.

Knapp, Bettina L. *Emily Dickinson*. New York: Continuum Publishing, 1989.

Knight, Denise D. "Oliver Wendell Holmes (1809–1894)," *Writers of the American Renaissance: An A-to-Z Guide*. Westport: Greenwood Publishing Group, 2003.

Lee, Hermione. *Willa Cather: Double Lives*. New York: Pantheon, 1989.

Lee, Hermione. *Edith Wharton*. New York: Knopf, 2007.

Leverich, Lyle. *Tom: The Unknown Tennessee Williams*. New York: W. W. Norton & Company, 1997.

Lewis, R.W.B. *Edith Wharton: A Biography*. New York: Harper & Row, 1975.

Liao Kang. *Pearl S. Buck: A Cultural Bridge Across the Pacific*. Westport: Greenwood Press, 1997.

Lingeman, Richard R. *Theodore Dreiser: An American Journey* (Abridged Edition). Hoboken: Wiley, 1993.

Lingeman, Richard R. *Sinclair Lewis: Rebel From Main Street*. Wadena: Borealis Books, 2002.

Loving, Jerome. *The Last Titan: A Life of Theodore Dreiser*. Berkeley: University of California Press, 2005.

Maher, Paul. *Kerouac: His Life and Work*. Latham: Taylor Trade Publishing, 2007.

Malcolm, Janet. *The Silent Woman: Sylvia Plath and Ted Hughes*. New York: Vintage, 1995.

Malcolm, Janet. *Two Lives: Gertrude and Alice*. New Haven: Yale University Press, 2007.

Matteson, John. *Eden's Outcasts: The Story of Louisa May Alcott and Her Father*. New York: W. W. Norton & Company, 2007.

May, Stephen J. *Zane Grey: Romancing The West*. Athens: Ohio University Press, 1997.

Maynard, Joyce. *At Home in the World*. New York: Picador, 1998.

McAleer, John. *Ralph Waldo Emerson: Days of Encounter*. Boston: Little, Brown and Company, 1984.

McFarland, Philip. *Hawthorne in Concord*. New York: Grove Press, 2004.

McFarland, Philip. *Loves of Harriet Beecher Stowe*. New York: Grove Press, 2007.

McNeil, Helen. *Emily Dickinson*. London: Virago Press, 1986.

Mellow, James R. *Charmed Circle: Gertrude Stein & Company*. New York: Praeger Publishers, 1974.

Mellow, James R. *Nathaniel Hawthorne in His Times*. Boston: Houghton Mifflin Company, 1980.

Mellow, James R. *Hemingway: A Life Without Consequences*. Boston: Houghton Mifflin, 1992.

Meltzer, Milton. *Carl Sandburg: A Biography*. Brookfield: Millbrook Press, 1999.

Meyers, Jeffrey. *Edgar Allan Poe: His Life and Legacy*. New York: Cooper Square Press, 1992.

Meyers, Jeffrey. *Hemingway: A Biography*. New York: Macmillan, 1995.

Meyers, Jeffrey. *Robert Frost: A Biography*. New York: Houghton Mifflin, 1996.

Milford, Nancy. *Zelda: A Biography*. New York: Harper & Row, 1970.

Miller, Arthur & Tony Kushner. *Arthur Miller: Collected Plays 1944-1961*. New York: Library of America, 2006.

Miller, Edwin Haviland. *Salem Is My Dwelling Place: A Life of Nathaniel Hawthorne*. Iowa City: University of Iowa Press, 1991.

Mizener, Arthur. *The Far Side of Paradise: A Biography of F. Scott Fitzgerald*. Boston: Houghton Mifflin, 1951.

Morgan, Judith and Neil Morgan. *Dr. Seuss & Mr. Geisel*. New York: Random House, 1995.

Moss, Leonard. *Arthur Miller*. Boston: Twayne Publishers, 1980.

Myerson, Joel. *A Historical Guide to Ralph Waldo Emerson*. New York: Oxford University Press, 2000.

New York Times. "O. Henry on Himself, Life, and Other Things." April 4, 1909.

New York Times. "Edith Wharton, 75 is Dead in France." August 13, 1937.

New York Times. "On This Day: Hemingway's Prize-Winning Works Reflected Preoccupation With Life and Death." http://www.nytimes.com/learning/general/onthisday/bday/0721.html. Accessed October 5, 2012.

Niven, Penelope. *Thornton Wilder: A Life*. New York: Harper, 2012.

O'Connor, Richard. *O.Henry: The Legendary*

Life of William S. Porter. New York: Doubleday, 1970.

Paradowski, Robert J. and Martha E. Rhynes. *Ray Bradbury*. Ipswich: Salem Press, 2001.

Parini, Jay. *John Steinbeck: A Biography*. New York: Henry Holt & Co., 1996.

Parini, Jay. *One Matchless Time: A Life of William Faulkner*. New York: HarperCollins, 2004.

Pauly, Thomas H. *Zane Grey: His Life, His Adventures, His Women*. Chicago: University of Illinois Press, 2005.

Pease, Donald E. *Theodor Seuss Geisel*. New York: Oxford Press, 2010.

Phillips, Mary Elizabeth. *James Fenimore Cooper*. London: John Lane Company, 1913.

Powers, Ron. *Dangerous Water: A Biography of the Boy Who Became Mark Twain*. New York: Da Capo Press, 1999.

Powers, Ron. *Mark Twain: A Life*. New York: Random House, 2005.

Pritchard, William H. *Updike: America's Man of Letters*. Amherst: University of Massachusetts Press, 2005.

Pyron, Darden Asbury. *Southern Daughter: The Life of Margaret Mitchell*. New York: Oxford University Press, 1991.

Reef, Catherine. *E.E. Cummings: A Poet's Life*. New York: Clarion Books, 2006.

Reesman, Jeanne Campbell. *Jack London's Racial Lives: A Critical Biography*. Athens: University of Georgia Press, 2009.

Reynolds, David S. *Walt Whitman's America: A Cultural Biography*. New York: Vintage Books, 1995.

Reynolds, Michael. *Hemingway: The 1930s through the Final Years*. New York: Norton, 1999.

Richardson, Jr., Robert D. *Henry Thoreau: A Life of the Mind*. Berkley: University of California Press, 1986.

Richardson, Jr., Robert D. *Emerson: The Mind on Fire*. Berkeley: University of California Press, 1995.

Riley, Michael O. *Oz and Beyond: The Fantasy World of L. Frank Baum*. Lawrence: University of Kansas Press, 1997.

Robertson-Lorant, Laurie. *Melville: A Biography*. New York: Clarkson Potter Publishers, 1996.

Rogers, Katharine M. L. *Frank Baum, Creator of Oz: A Biography*. New York: St. Martin's Press, 2002.

Salinger, Margaret. *Dream Catcher: A Memoir*. New York: Washington Square Press, 2000.

Sawyer-Lauçanno, Christopher. *E.E. Cummings: A Biography*. Naperville: Sourcebooks, Inc., 2004.

Saxton, Martha. *Louisa May: A Modern Biography of Louisa May Alcott*. Boston: Houghton Mifflin, 1977.

Schorer, Mark. *Sinclair Lewis: An American Life*. New York: McGraw-Hill, 1961.

Sensibar, Judith L. *Faulkner and Love: The Women Who Shaped His Art, A Biography*. New Haven: Yale University Press, 2008.

Sewall, Richard B. *The Life of Emily Dickinson*. New York: Farrar, Strauss, and Giroux, 1974.

Sheaffer, Louis. *O'Neill: Son and Artist*. New York: Little, Brown & Co., 1973.

Shields, Charles. *And So It Goes: Kurt Vonnegut: A Life*. New York: Henry Holt, 2007.

Silverman, Kenneth. *Edgar A. Poe: Mournful and Never-Ending Remembrance*. New York: Harper Perennial, 1991.

Simpson, Melissa. *Flannery O'Connor: A Biography*. Westport: Greenwood Press, 2005.

Sova, Dawn B. *Edgar Allan Poe A to Z: The Essential Reference to His Life and Work* (Paperback ed.). New York: Checkmark Books, 2001.

Spoto, Donald. *The Kindness of Strangers: The Life of Tennessee Williams*. Cambridge: Da Capo Press, 1997.

Stallman, R. W. *Stephen Crane: A Biography*. New York: Braziller, Inc., 1968.

Stasz, Clarice. *Jack London's Women*. Amherst: University of Massachusetts Press, 2001.

Sumner, Gregory. *Unstuck in Time: A Journey Through Kurt Vonnegut's Life and Novels*. New York: Seven Stories Press, 2011.

Thompson, Lawrence. *Young Longfellow (1807–1843)*. New York: The Macmillan Company, 1938.

151

Tilton, Eleanor M. *Amiable Autocrat: A Biography of Dr. Oliver Wendell Holmes*. New York: H. Schuman, 1947.

Updike, John. *Self-Consciousness: Memoir*. New York: Random House, 2012.

Wagenknecht, Edward. *Henry Wadsworth Longfellow: Portrait of an American Humanist*. New York: Oxford University Press, 1966.

Walsh, John Evangelist. *The Hidden Life of Emily Dickinson*. New York: Simon and Schuster, 1971.

Eugene Walter and Ralph Ellison. "Robert Penn Warren, The Art of Fiction, No. 18." *The Paris Review*. http://www.theparisreview. org/interviews/4868/the-art-of-fiction-no-18-robert-penn-warren. Accessed October 5, 2012.

Weller, Sam. *The Bradbury Chronicles: The Life of Ray Bradbury*. New York: HarperCollins, 2005.

Wertheim, Stanley and Paul Sorrentino. *The Crane Log: A Documentary Life of Stephen Crane, 1871-1900*. New York: G. K. Hall & Co., 1994.

Williams, Cecil B. *Henry Wadsworth Longfellow*. New York: Twayne Publishers, 1964.

Williams, Stanley T. *The Life of Washington Irving*. New York: Oxford University Press, 1935.

Williams, Tennessee. *Memoirs*. New York: Doubleday, 1975.

Wineapple, Brenda. "Song of Himself." *New York Times*, August 10, 2003, http://www. nytimes.com/2003/08/10/books/song-of-himself.html. Accessed October 4, 2012.

Wineapple, Brenda. *Hawthorne: A Life*. New York: Random House, 2003.

Wolff, Cynthia Griffin. *Emily Dickinson*. New York: Alfred A. Knopf, 1986.

Woodress, James Leslie. *Willa Cather: A Literary Life*. Omaha: University of Nebraska Press, 1987.

Adams, Samuel, 8

Alcott, Bronson, 16, 21, 35, 47

Alcott, Louisa May, 16-17, 47-48

Allan, John, 25-26

Appleton, Francis Elizabeth "Fanny", 23

Anderson, Clara Mathilda, 87

Angell, Katharine, 112

Bacheller, Irving, 55-56

Balzac, Honre de, 13

Barley, Agnes, 127

Barnett, Augusta, 126

Barton, Anne, 96

Baum, Benjamin Ward, 62

Baum, Lyman Frank, 62-63

Becker, Charles, 55-56

Beecher, Henry Ward, 34

Beecher, Lyman, 32

Bernhard, Martha Ruggles, 146

Bianchi, Martha Dickinson, 46

Bingham, Millicent Todd, 46

Boak, Mary Virginia, 71

Boulton, Agnes, 92

Bradbury, Leonard Spaulding, 131

Bradbury, Ray, 131-132

Bradstreet, Anne, 6

Brescia, Emma, 121

Brett, George Platt, 85

Brown, John, 36

Brown, William Hill, 8

Brown, William Slater, 95

Buck, John Lossing, 94-94

Buck, Pearl S., 93-94

Burroughs, Edgar Rice, 82-83

Burroughs, George Tyler, 82

Burroughs, William, 136

Bush, George W., 134

Butler, Maud, 101

Capote, Joe, 138

Capote, Truman, 61, 138-139

Carlyle, Thomas, 15

Carpenter, Meta, 102

Carr, Lucien, 136

Carson, Joanne, 139

Carson, Johnny, 139

Cassady, Neal, 135

Cather, Charles Fectigue, 71

Cather, Willa, 60, 71-72, 90

Chaney, John Griffith (see Jack London), 84-86

Chaney, William, 84

Channing, Ellery, 20, 37

Chaplin, Charlie, 92

Chapman, Mark David, 129-130

Clark, Dora, 55

Clarke, Rebecca Haswell, 95

Clemens, John Marshall, 49

Clemens, Samuel (see Mark Twain), 49-51

Clemm, Maria, 26, 27

Clemm, Virginia Eliza, 26

Cline, Regina, 140

Coleridge, Samuel Taylor, 15

Conger, Gwendolyn, 117

Cooper, James Fenimore, 8, 12-14

Cooper, Susan Fenimore, 13

Copper, William, 12

Cox, Jane Marie, 133

Crane, Jonathan Townley, 54

Crane, Stephen, 9, 54-57

Cudlip, Thelma, 69

Cummings, E.E., 60, 95-96

Cummings, Edward, 95

Dakin, Edwina, 123

Day-Lewis, Daniel, 127

Dearholt, Ashton, 83

Delancey, Susan Augusta, 13

Dickens, Charles, 27, 50

Dickinson, Edward, 44-46

Dickinson, Emily, 6, 44-46

Dickinson, John, 8

Dickinson, Samuel Fowler, 44

Dimond, Audrey Stone, 120

Douglas, Claire, 129

Dos Passos, John, 95, 107

Dreiser, John Paul, 68

Dreiser, Theodore, 69-70, 90, 122

Dunbar, Cynthia, 35

Dunphy, Jack, 139

Eddy, Mary Baker, 71

Edwards, Jonathan, 8

Eliot, T.S., 60

Emerson, Ellen, 17, 48

Emerson, Ralph Waldo, 9, 15-17, 20-21, 31, 35, 37, 42, 45, 47-48, 52

Emerson, William, 15

Estes, Athol, 64-65

Falkner, Murry Cuthbert, 101

Faulk, Lillie Mae, 138

Faulkner, William, 60-61, 101-103

Fenimore, Elizabeth, 12

Ferrand, Beatrix, 67

Fields, James Thomas, 19, 21

Fitzgerald, Edward, 97

Fitzgerald, F. Scott, 60, 66, 74, 97-100, 110

Fitzgerald, Frances Scott "Scottie", 90, 100

Fitzgerald, Zelda (see Zelda Sayre), 98-100

Foote, Roxanna, 32

Ford, John, 117

Franklin, Benjamin, 8

French, Daniel Chester, 17

Freneau, Philip, 7

Frost, Robert, 60, 76-78

Frost, William Prescott, 76

Fuller, Margaret, 16, 35, 47

Gage, Matilda Joslyn, 63

Gage, Maud, 63-64

Ganservort, Maria, 38

Gaylord, Winfield P., 87

Geisel, Theodor Robert, 119

Geisel, Theodor Seuss (see Dr. Seuss), 119-120

Gellhorn, Martha, 109-111

Gilbert, Florence, 83

Gilbert, Susan, 45

Gillette, Chester, 69

Ginsberg, Allen, 135

Graham, Sheilah, 99

Gravitt, Hugh, 115

Gray, Lewis, 79

Gray, Romer "Reddy", 79

Grey, Zane, 79-81

Griswold, Rufus Wilmot, 27

Hall, Ernest, 106

Hall, Grace, 106

Hamilton, Olive, 116

Hart, Jessie, 112

Haskins, Ruth, 15

Hathorne, John, 18

Hathorne, Nathaniel Sr., 18

Haverty, Joan, 136

Hawthorne, Nathaniel, 9, 16-21, 23, 39, 47

Hawthorne, Una, 21

Hearst, William Randolph, 56

Hegger, Grace Livingston, 90

Henning, Carol, 116

Hemingway, Clarence Edmonds, 106

Hemingway, Ernest, 51, 54-55, 60, 74, 90, 99, 106-111, 129

Henry, O. (see William Sydney Porter), 64-65

Higginson, Thomas Wentworth, 45-46

Hinkley, John Jr., 129

Hoffman, Matilda, 10

Holbrook, Josiah, 16

Holmes, Abiel, 29

Holmes, John Clellon, 135

Holmes, Oliver Wendell Jr., 30

Holmes, Oliver Wendell Sr., 9, 21, 29-31, 38

Hopkins, Elizabeth Arnold, 25

Hopkinson, Francis, 8

Hoyer, Linda Grace, 145

Hughes, Ted, 142-143

Hulbert, Emma, 82

Hungerford, Margaret Wolfe, 4

Irving, Washington, 4, 8, 10-11

Irving, William, 10

Ivancich, Adriana, 110

Jackson, Charles, 30

Jackson, Amelia Lee, 30

Jackson, Lydia, 16

James, Henry, 9, 52-53

James, Henry Sr., 52

James, William, 53, 73, 95

Jenkins, Kathleen, 91,

Jillich, Marie, 128

Johnson, Lyndon, 118

Jones, Edith Newbold (see Edith Wharton), 66-67

Jones, George Fredric, 66

Joyce, Elaine, 130

Joyce, James, 74, 110, 129

Kennedy, John F., 77, 105

Kermott, Emma, 89

Kerouac, Jack, 61, 135-137

Kerouac, Janet, 137

Kerouac, Leo, 135

Kittredge, Charmian, 85

Krammerer, David, 136

Krementz, Jill, 133

Kurkowsky, Agnes von, 107

Lampton, Jane, 49

Langdon, Charles, 50

Langdon, Olivia, 50

Lee, Harper, 121, 138-139

Lennon, John, 129

Levesque, Gabrielle, 135

Lewis, Edwin J., 89

Lewis, Sinclair, 89-90

Lieber, Edith, 133

Lincoln, Abraham, 33, 87-88

Little, Lou, 135

London, Jack (see John Griffith Chaney), 9, 84-86

Long, Huey P., 122

Longfellow, Henry Wadsworth, 9, 11, 18, 20-24, 28

Longfellow, Stephen, 22

Lowell, Amy, 95-96

Lowell, Robert, 143

Lytle, Andrew, 140

Maddern, Bessie, 85

Manning, Elizabeth Clarke, 18

Manrique, Jorge, 23

Marsh, John R., 114

Mather, Cotton, 7

Matisse, Henri, 74

Mav, Abigail, 47

Maynard, Joyce, 129-130

McClure, Marguerite, 132

McNeill, Hammond, 57

McQuillan, Mollie, 97

Melvill, Allan, 38

Melvill, Thomas, 38

Melville, Herman, 9, 20, 38-40, 60, 122

Merlo, Frank Phillip, 124

Miller, Arthur, 126-127, 146

Miller, Isidore, 126

Miller, Rebecca, 127

Mitchell, Eugene Muse, 114

Mitchell, Margaret, 114-115

Moberg, Esther, 131

Monroe, Marilyn, 127

Montenegro, Brenda, 80

Monterey, Carlotta, 92

Moodie, Isabella, 76

Morath, Ingeborg, 127

Morehouse, Marion, 96

Niven, Isabella, 104

Norcross, Emily, 44

O'Connor, Edwin, 140

O'Connor, Flannery, 61, 140-141

O'Neill, Colleen, 130

O'Neill, Eugene, 91-92

O'Neill, James, 91

O'Neill, Oona, 92

O'Neill, Shane, 92

Oldham, Estelle, 102

Orr, Elaine, 96

Paine, Thomas, 8

Palmer, Helen, 119

Parker, Edie, 136

Patterson, Louisa, 26

Peabody, Elizabeth, 19, 36

Peabody, Sophia, 19

Peck, Mary Helen, 54

Penn, Anna, 121

Perkins, Maxwell, 98-110

Persons, Archulus, 138

Pfeiffer, Pauline, 108-109, 111

Picasso, Pablo, 74

Pierce, Franklin, 18, 20-21

Plath, Otto, 142

Plath, Sylvia, 142-144

Poe, David, 25

Poe, Edgar Allan, 9, 25-28, 131

Polk, James K., 39

Porter, Algernon Sidney, 64

Porter, Evelina Maria, 64

Porter, William Sydney (see O. Henry), 64-65

Potter, Mary Storer, 23

Pound, Ezra, 60, 74, 96

Quinlan, Mary Ellen, 91

Reagan, Ronald, 129

Reed, John, 91

Rhinelander, Lucretia, 66

Richardson, Hadley, 108-109, 111

Ricketts, Edward, 117

Rogers, Henry Huttleston, 51

Romulo, Carlos, 94

Ripley, Ezra, 16

Roth, Lina "Dolly", 80

Royce, Josiah, 95

Salinger, J.D., 61, 128-130

Salinger, Sol, 128

Sampas, Stella, 137

Sandburg, August, 87

Sandburg, Carl, 87-88

Sanders, Sarah, 10

Sayre, Zelda (see Zelda Fitzgerald), 98-100

Schanab, Sarah Maria, 68

Schober, Aurelia, 142

Scott, Elaine, 117

Seuss, Dr. (see Theodor Geisel), 119-120

Seuss, Henrietta, 119

Sexton, Anne, 143

Shaw, Elizabth, 39

Shaw, Lemuel, 39

Smith, John, 6

Stanton, Cynthia Ann, 62

Steichen, Eduard (Edward), 87

Steichen, Lilian, 87-88

Stein, Amelia, 73

Stein, Daniel, 73

Stein, Gertrude, 60, 73-75, 96, 99, 105, 108, 110

Steinbeck, John, 60, 116-118

Steinbeck, John Ernst, 116

Stephens, Mary Isabele, 114

Steward, Samuel, 105

St. John, John Hector, 7

Stowe, Calvin Ellis, 33

Stowe, Harriet Beecher, 32-34

Strunk, William Jr., 113

Strunsky, Anna, 85

Stulting, Caroline, 93

Swain, Mary Jane, 64

Sydenstricker, Absalom, 93

Taylor, Cora, 56-57

Taylor, Edward, 7

Tennyson, Alfred Lord, 28

Thompson, Dorothy, 90

Thoreau, Henry David, 16-17, 20, 35-37, 47, 52

Thoreau, John, 35

Todd, Mabel Loomis, 46

Toklas, Alice B., 73-75

Tolstoy, Leo, 13

Trumbull, John, 8

Tucker, Ellen Louisa, 15

Twain, Mark (see Samuel Clemens), 9, 49-51, 60

Updike, John, 61, 145-146

Updike, Wesley Russell, 145

Upshaw, Berrien "Red", 114

VVan, Bobby, 130

Van Velsor, Louisa, 41

Vonnegut, Kurt Jr., 60, 133-134

Vonnegut, Kurt Sr., 133

Wadsworth, Zilpah, 22

Walsh, Mary Robertson, 52

Walsh, Richard J., 94

Warren, Robert, 121

Warren, Robert Penn, 60, 121-122, 140

Wellman, Flora, 84

Welsh, Mary, 110

Welter, Sylvia, 129

Wendell, Sarah, 29

Wevill Assiaz, 143

Wevill, David, 143

Wharton, Edith (see Edith Newbold Jones), 66-67

Wharton, Edward Robbins, 66

Wheatley, Phillis, 7

Whipple, Edwin Percy, 21

Whistler, Anna McNeill, 57

White, E.B., 112-113

White, Elinor Miriam, 76

White, Samuel Tilly, 112

White, Sarah Osborne, 68-69

Whitman, Walt, 9, 28, 41-43, 60, 87

Whitman, Walter Sr., 41

Wilder, Amos Parker, 104

Wilder, Thornton, 104-105

Williams, Cornelius, 123

Williams, Joan, 102

Williams, Tennessee, 123-125

Wilson, Woodrow, 91

Wood, Audrey, 124

Wordsworth, William, 15

Zane, Alice Josephine, 79

Ziegler, Mary Evaline, 82

Legends Never Die